MONEY SIGNS

Fredrick Davies is a[n] [...] [be]come famous on both sid[es...] [pers]onal astrologer to many [...] for national newspapers [...] [Uni]t[ed] [St]ates including *Vogue* and [...] [Hi]s television work includes the imm[ense...] *Fredrick Davies Star Power Show* in New Y[ork], and *Star Signs* for the BBC. He now lives in America.

Paul Bannister is a journalist and the author of a survey of occult phenomena. He has travelled the world as senior reporter specialising in parapsychology for America's largest newspaper, and has written a book on astrology. He is English, and now lives in California.

Jeane Dixon is America's leading seer who forecast the deaths of the Kennedy brothers and the financial upheavals of the last decade. She has raised several millions of dollars for a children's charity and is a national celebrity in the United States.

MONEY SIGNS

Fredrick Davies and Paul Bannister

A STAR BOOK

published by
the Paperback Division Bof
W. H. ALLEN & Co. Ltd

A Star Book
Published in 1981
by the Paperback Division of
W. H. Allen & Co. Ltd
A Howard and Wyndham Company
44 Hill Street, London W1X 8LB

First published in Great Britain by Star Books

Typeset by V & M Graphics, Aylesbury, Bucks
Printed in Great Britain by
Hunt Barnard Printing Ltd, Aylesbury, Bucks

ISBN 0 352 30809 5

Contents

Foreword

We talk of business acumen, of hunches, flashes of inspiration and of heightened awareness in our daily lives – but how often do we realise that what we regard as a lightning flash of intuition is really a demonstration of a constant, ever-present psychic ability?

This book is concerned with the marriage of practical business techniques and nebulous psychic functioning, using astrology only as a focusing tool. I am sure that it will demonstrate to the careful reader that consciousness does indeed work at many levels.

I have spent a lifetime refining the gifts God gave me, gifts of psychic ability. I have studied astrology just as I have studied business practice, and I believe each is valid. If we can know how the unseen influences that act on us all affect us, we can be better and more valuable people.

Science will soon discover the keys to understanding some of those subtle astrological influences upon us. On that day, we will be closer to a more perfect understanding of ourselves and of the wonderful creation God has made.

Jeane Dixon, Washington, DC
June 1981

Chapter One
Your financial personality

'Whenever you think you are about to be able to make both ends meet, somebody moves the ends.'

Anonymous

People who come to me for astrological readings constantly ask the same questions. Love, health, opportunities and money are the favourite topics. And today I hear more and more often the demand, 'How can I make my money go further?'

There is no easy answer, of course, but I believe that as long as people are influenced by others and influence others in turn, then knowing your own strengths and weaknesses can help you manage your financial affairs better.

It is like going on a diet. At some stage we all make fierce resolutions and set out determined to eat less and exercise more but after a day or two we get hungry, become bored, give in to temptation or simply rebel and the new regime that was going to change our lives goes out of the window.

Behaviour modification is rarely something that can be achieved dramatically quickly. We are usually most successful when we take things a step at a time, reinforcing our gains – or weight losses – as we make them, one by one.

This book will show you how you can use your inherent astrological strengths to become a better money manager. Step by step you can see what you can do, what opportunities are best suited to your personality and how you can go about managing your financial business either day by day or decades ahead. I hope you'll find it down to earth advice that comes from the heavens.

Let's start with a brief look at the traits of each astrological sign.

ARIES (21st March – 19th April)

Aggressive Ariens, loaded with ego, enthusiasm, wonder and enjoyment of life are nimble of brain, bursting with drive and constantly in search of some new and testing project on which to try their astrological horns.

Aries folk feel that a letter can be left unanswered for a week or two – because they have important, urgent things to be doing first. Then they remember it, and rather than be bogged down in the everyday task of answering it, reason that if it could wait a couple of weeks already, why bother to answer it at all?

They are not careless, just frequently preoccupied. Rams tend to wear out their colleagues and friends. They involve themselves in dozens of business projects and enterprises, knowing that they can bring their fine talents to bear – but forgetting that the few minutes of effort they can afford to put in, or the few minutes that the project will hold their attention, really is not enough.

So life can be a procession of unfinished enterprises for them – which is as frustrating for the Ariens involved as it is for those with whom they are working.

Yet the Aries in business can be at a decided advantage once he learns to spend more time on fewer projects. That unstoppable drive and unquenchable enthusiasm can set the whole project on fire, and boost the morale and efforts of anyone who is sharing in the enterprise.

A recent survey of the characteristics of self-made men showed they had all the Aries traits: they were strong-willed, they learned from life, they had lives of gathering purpose and drive. In fact, many of them found that formal schooling was a negative influence on them – and they included such luminaries as Wilbur Wright, the illiterate Pablo Picasso and the kitchen-table tinkerer Thomas Edison.

All these successful people suffered setbacks at some stage, but carried on regardless developing their skills through active, getting-out-and-doing-it techniques. And that's Aries' strength, and the key to his money-making success.

It can be a reason for Aries losing money because sometimes, in blind stubbornness, he'll carry on long after a cooler-headed person would have turned aside from a losing venture. It isn't anything to worry about, though – that Arien drive will always set up other opportunities.

Here are a few more adjectives to help the typical Arien understand his own personality: headstrong, quick witted, enterprising, easily roused, swift to forgive. Ariens hate to be under the direction of someone else and are easy to sway because of their extremes of enthusiasm. Sometimes they lack discretion, they can be outspoken, they love adventure and they are intensely loyal.

They are good at accumulating goods and get a lot for their money but tend not to realise the value of what they own. Ariens generally are not very interested in making money, are active in sports, love anything military and really only find a use for money in that it can buy them freedom to do what they really want – be it splashing out on an expensive meal or going for a fast drive. They value that sense of freedom to indulge today's whim.

This can be a major weakness in money matters. It means that Ariens are especially vulnerable to the four-colour glossy brochure for a gold-plated toothpick, to the 'special offer' and the sporting goods store's gimmick sale.

Ariens tend to make plenty of money – but it trickles away quickly through their generous hands as they splash out on lavish gifts for friends, on tools they will never use and on clothing they will rarely wear.

It means that those born under the sign of the Ram should be especially careful of mail order offers and of credit cards. Arm an Arien with a wallet full of shiny plastic and watch him rapidly turn his bank statement from black to red.

Far better for the Arien to shed all but one credit card and carry a pocket full of cash or traveller's cheques. That way he can see how the money flows away – it's much more personal than a hastily-scribbled signature on a restaurant bill when he's full of wine.

Another financial minefield for the Arien comes when he has to collect from people who owe him money. Face to face, he is a soft touch for a sob story and if he doesn't impulsively cancel the debt, he is extremely likely to defer payment of it.

So, when it is time to call in the debt, the Arien should write a polite letter. A letter pointing out that the debtor owes the money and asking if perhaps he is having difficulty in repaying it is always helpful. That way, you can appear concerned yet firm, and a letter is always more businesslike than a stammering telephone conversation.

Equally, when Ariens owe money, instead of ignoring the fact, they can always write a letter explaining that they have not forgotten the debt, are presently taking certain steps to repay it and thank the creditor for his patience. It's reassuring from either end to have communication.

So the bottom line of this astrological balance sheet of the Ariens' personality is that they are subject to impulse buying. Recognise that, and you are more than halfway to solving the problem.

They should always shop with a shopping list and only buy from a mail order catalogue after careful consideration. They should try not to use credit cards or hire purchase and be wary of 'special offers'. Careful shoppers aren't stampeded into buying something they probably don't really want anyway.

TAURUS (20th April – 21st May)
Loveable, stubborn, bull-headed Taurus, popularly seen as being dogmatic and practical, determined and materialistic – this book was written for you. For Taureans are untiring in

their efforts to do more for others, and practical enough to know that a good cash flow is a useful tool to achieve this end.

Taurean traits include thoroughness, conservatism, thrift and industry. The local banker is probably a Taurean because this is the money sign of the Zodiac. Taureans are generous and affectionate, civic-minded, often musically inclined and most creative. They make good specialists at almost any endeavour because they are retentive and determined.

Sometimes, especially in romantic matters, Taureans tend to hang on longer than they should – their inherent stubbornness means they rarely like to make an exit, however graceful.

They're stable yet secretive, sensual and possessive. Taureans are creatures of strong appetite, for both sexual adventure and for experiences in the outside world. They love routine and the comfortable rut, yet are surprisingly ready to begin an adventure. They are also sympathetic people and sometimes a trifle vain. They are generally intelligent and often lazy because they can work out how best to allow themselves that indulgence. Some rare Taureans work hard and do extremely well. Generally, however, they prefer not to take on the often onerous duties of being a leader and would rather follow some adventurous Aries or Leo and tidy up their mistakes, comforted in the knowledge that they could have easily done a better, if less venturesome, job in the first place ...

They handle money well because they are respectable and responsible and a cornerstone of the Zodiac. More bankers, mortgage brokers and savings institution officers are Taureans than any pollster would believe – it's a natural affinity Taureans have for money. They are as solid as the Bank of England and generally are held in similar esteem.

For Taureans, their patterns of life are laid quickly. Usually doting aunts and uncles dropped gifts of money into their first pink piggy bank and the tiny Taureans were brought up gurgling happily to the sound of jingling coins. Most Taureans start life as the kids whose clothes are always neat and clean and grow up to become the responsible, slightly solemn young parent in the 'steady' job, whose adult success is as undramatic as it is inevitable. And through it all they have that enviable ability to handle money. Nobody ever seems to instruct Taureans, they just know by instinct which sales are genuine and where the best bargains are.

So what and where are their weaknesses? It is hard to say for they balance their cheque books, manage their credit cards, make regular savings deposits and pay their bills on time. They are disciplined and practical people who rarely marry before they have organised their new home, new furniture and career prospects.

However there is a chink in all this polished armour. Taureans are sensual creatures, great and passionate lovers. It is as if they shed their inhibitions with their respectable suits and a common weakness among Taurus people is that they are hopeless romantics. They will spend money on lovers as if there is no tomorrow, lavishing gifts and entertainments to woo their new love.

Taureans tend to be in love with love itself, and put no financial limitations on it. The cool-headed, pragmatic person behind the cashbox at the bank becomes a sensual creature who will use all his economic clout to achieve his goal. It can mean that debts are incurred that shouldn't be; that credit card charges are run up heedlessly and that cheques are written like confetti – until the Taurean descends from Cloud Nine.

Here are some other, lesser weaknesses to guard against: Taureans love to buy objets d'art; often they will be fine investments, sometimes they will be simply beautiful – and horribly expensive. They will override their own inclinations of prudence to possess them – so beware.

Some Taureans are obsessively concerned about their health, and it's usually unwarranted. Consult a loved one before you start wasting a doctor's time – and incurring expense. Often the advice of a close friend will put matters in a new perspective.

Taureans should not regard unpaid debts of others as personal insults against themselves. Because Taureans are so careful to discharge debts promptly they expect others to do the same and when some don't they think of it as an insult. Simply send a brief letter or make a friendly telephone call to remind the debtor – legal action is rarely needed.

One other weakness: Taurus folk are very hospitable, and love to entertain at home. Usually this is partly because their homes are showplaces, tastefully furnished and full of expensive objects and partly because there the Taurus cook can show off his skill at preparing the rich dishes he loves. However, this entertaining can be expensive and sometimes overwhelming for guests who have neither the time nor inclination to go to such lengths to reciprocate. Entertain by all means – but sometimes make the evening a simple one instead of a Technicolor production.

Many Taureans could benefit from a little more exercise and a little less food – so consider going for a walk now and then, or taking a bicycle ride instead of visiting a theatre or cinema or restaurant. Make yourself slimmer, and your bank account fatter.

GEMINI (22nd May – 6th June)
Quicksilver Gemini, the people who put the twin in twinkle, are the mental gymnasts of the Zodiac. They're talkative, witty, funloving and changeable. Money doesn't usually play a dominant role in their lives because they rightly regard it as something which mysteriously arrives just when they need it most.

Their very duality of personality means, however, that they can be thrifty and cautious yesterday, prodigal and abandoned today. They aren't money managers, hate to plan ahead and are not usually driven too hard by any thought that they need to get money.

Geminis are cerebral people, adaptable, alert, restless and with a continuing lively interest in the world and its people. They're dexterous, geared to manual skills like needlework and painting and often have great powers of expression and communication.

Another set of traits owned by a majority of those born under the sign of the Twins is that they are caring, sensitive people who make good mediators. They are tolerant of others in an easy way, are open-minded and are responsive to the needs of others.

The other side of the Gemini coin is that they are sometimes anxious, indecisive and impatient. Their nimble minds skip around all sides of a problem, choose first one solution then another, confuse themselves – and any listeners – then take off on some more interesting tangent.

When they are involved and feeling responsible, they can be very protective and caring, very cautious and forward-looking, but it generally only lasts for a short time. They are subject to brief and explosive interludes, when they stir up a storm, batter less volatile mortals into submission or anger, then settle into unruffled calm. It's very frustrating, as the slower-to-anger people are usually left simmering, while the Gemini provocateur is all sweetness and light.

Their quick wits can be a tremendous business asset, if they can be harnessed long enough for them to have real effects, but generally Geminis have shorter attention and concentration spans, in the style of their Arien cousins, and the mere business of making money doesn't appeal to them once they have demonstrated to themselves that they can.

Life for Geminis is a puzzling patchwork, a jigsaw puzzle of black, white some greys and a whole rainbow of bright colours. They will argue and complain, charm and advocate, contradict and stimulate. They will set out to make a fortune one day selling cosmetics, or property or mail order and they will have everything running smoothly within a surprisingly small number of days, thanks to their tremendous energy and dedication at the start of this exciting new enterprise.

But a month later, the Twins will be looking around elsewhere. They'll decide that mail order has no future, that antiques are the coming thing, that cosmetics are old hat and that property is too dull. So they'll launch off into electronics, or selling farm equipment – anything as long as it is different, and off they'll go, leaving some poor Taurean of Libran holding the baby.

They have no inclination to handle money, so usually they'll settle for a business partnership with someone who can.

It is a problem, but it is also a strength. It means that they aren't hoarders of money, they regard it as of relatively little importance. It is convenient – and they love to use money for travel, for exciting new experiences. They spend on books and newspapers and magazines. They spend extravagantly on long-distance telephone calls, on posting newspaper cuttings and artistic little knick-knacks to their sometimes bemused friends.

They can be thrifty and even parsimonious one day, extravagant the next. They rarely have major difficulties with overspending – they simply spend on things that other people don't regard as necessary, yet they somehow manage to fumble along without owing too much to anybody, or being owed too much by anybody, either.

They will spend wildly on book club subscriptions, on maps and paintings, yet do without meals or clothes to keep solvent.

Geminis love travel, and will think nothing of wildly overspending on air tickets to bask in the sunshine for a long weekend. Frequently, Geminis have better than average cars, because they enjoy the sensation of being able to up stakes and dash away for a few days, throwing a suitcase, the family pet and the children in the back of the car and ignoring the weekend chores, school meeting and impending visit of relatives.

They make bad debtors because it isn't usually important to them to repay money – and they are frankly astonished that it is so important to a bank or loan company that the money should be repaid promptly. Check any Gemini's desk top – it's invariably host to a handful of unpaid bills.

Equally, it is relatively unimportant to them to claim money that's owing. They tend to adopt the attitude that people will pay them when it's convenient, and usually that's what happens. Geminis lose little sleep over debts – outstanding or unpaid.

Geminis and credit make uneasy bedfellows, though. A Gemini with a wallet filled with shiny plastic is too unstable, too likely to take off and overspend and not be able to repay for months and months. This is one Zodiac sign who really should use cash, and only cash, for purchases. It's even dangerous for many Geminis to have a bank account – it is far too easy for them to sign a piece of paper and hang the consequences.

They are generous tippers, love to be gregarious and are popular in bars where they think nothing of emptying their pockets on to the counter then watching it all disappear as they buy drinks for their more cautious friends; they are impulse buyers who should never be allowed loose without a prepared shopping list and they are generous gift-givers, often despite their own straitened circumstances.

Geminis, happily for them, often have several minor sources of income. It suits their personality to hold down several jobs and thus bring in extra cash – but it's often a case of easy come, easy go. Usually they are saved by forming a business partnership or a marriage with a complementary member of the Zodiac who harnesses and channels their energies and helps protect them from their own impulsive nature.

CANCER (21st June – 22nd July)

Here's one of the great money signs of the Zodiac – that of Cancer, the Crab. Sometimes called Moon Children, Cancer people are closely related to silver, the substance ruled by the moon. And it is an admirable parallel. Silver is practical yet aesthetic, valuable yet not so valuable as gold, malleable yet hard, cold yet beautiful.

Cancer is a water sign, and the moon on water has that silvery sheen so popular with songwriters, poets and Moon Children. Even the world's greatest silver discovery in modern history, that of the fabled Comstock Lode, in Nevada, was made in 1856, the year Saturn began to transit Cancer.

Those born under Cancer possess an interesting potpourri of traits. They are born money managers because money is important to them. However much they have, they seek more. Yet they do it for a purpose. They need money as a silvery security blanket.

Cancerians are emotional, maternal, patriotic, imaginative, impressionable, artistic and as retentive as the crab whose claws lock on to its enemies. They are also cautious, domestic, protective, intuitive and sympathetic. They are self-indulgent, possessive, clannish, brooding, frivolous, touchy, timid and dreamy.

Moon Children like money, work hard for it and hang on to it. They see it as a tool to allow them to build a secure domestic life, and believe the only real use for money is to provide themselves, and especially their families, with comfort and a haven.

Ask any Cancerian about his bank balance and he'll know exactly what is in it – although he might not tell you. He is constantly planning and scheming to use his money, is always aware of the state of his assets and lies awake wondering how to improve them.

Cancerians make cautious investors and shoppers. They are fussy, will read all the consumer guides, scan the classified advertisements and window shop for months before making a purchase. They hate to sell any of their possessions, even if it means buying new and better ones to replace the old. They feel great pangs of pain when they trade in their beloved old car for a new one. And so they should – they have probably lavished weeks cleaning and polishing, fiddling with it and tuning it, as it's an extension of their home.

Look in a Cancerian's photograph album. You'll probably find more pictures of their homes and cars than of themselves. There will be lots of pictures of their family, because they come first, but few of the Moon Child – because he is shy and somewhat self-effacing.

They handle money well because they are aware of its power. They prepare budgets, make shopping lists, clip coupons from magazines to get small discounts, buy the right things at the right times for bargains and love to window shop. Yet they dislike clothes shopping, and frequently have cupboards full of clothes bought without care which don't fit, or are the wrong colour. They are happiest when slopping around the home in a half-unravelled cardigan and carpet slippers.

Where credit purchases are concerned, they are meticulous. They use credit cards and mail order catalogues, keep their cheque books up to date (the person who holds you up in the supermarket line while she fills in her cheque book stub is usually Cancerian) and tend to ignore the facilities offered by revolving credit accounts. They pay up in full every month, usually on the same date – the first day of the new month.

When there is a special offer in the mail, the Cancerian householder will sit down and read all the literature carefully, even if the goods on offer have no appeal for him. He'll make comparisons, find smugly that he can get a better deal elsewhere – then throw away the special offer literature.

Does Cancer, you wonder, have a weakness? Indeed, yes. And the weakness of this closet hedonist is food. Cancerians invariably overbuy food. They will go to the supermarket and buy twice as much as they need, gloating secretly at having far more than enough. They have a feeling that they must have cupboards full of food, that they should be prepared for any emergency. Cancerians always want to feed people. They won't make one pie, but two or three, one for a neighbour, one for a daughter and so on. They would rather give food away than anything else, and they love to entertain guests to dinner parties.

At the end of a social evening at a Cancerian household, don't be surprised to have them thrust food upon you. 'Won't you take this home for later – we'd hate to waste it' will be the refrain.

They don't like to be indebted to anyone, either, and are scrupulous about making prompt repayments of any loan. When people owe them money, they fret and fuss over it. They constantly assess how much they would have if only so and so would pay up; they make bad creditors (although they invite trouble by being open-handed and over-generous sometimes to the point of forcing money on a friend or relative).

The message is clear. If you are a Cancerian, don't lend money. It isn't worth the heartache, even though you like to worry. Think that by hardening your soft heart and not lending out money you are protecting your family from possible hard times – and it will be easier for you.

Generally, however, Cancerians don't have money problems although they do enjoy their money worries, which are usually more imagined than real. Accept that your money isn't a real problem, and enjoy your domestic life – that's Cancer's best role, and their most enjoyable one.

LEO (23rd July – 22nd August)
The golden sign of the Zodiac, Leo is the flamboyant showman, the extrovert regal Lion. Leo is the sign of the Sun, the ruler of gold, the ultimate money sign.

And those centre-stage Leos know it. They're show-offs,

confident and assertive, superior and generous, affectionate and ardent. They are vital and vivacious, honourable and humble, determined, fearless, noble and commanding. They are the kings of the Zodiac, the imperious rulers whose ambition and ability often overshadows lesser mortals around them.

They know about money, but tend to treat it with the disdain that any royal, accustomed to its presence, can show. They can be spendthrift, they can be selfish, too. For Leos have great vanity, can be overbearing and conceited, contemptuous and cruel. They can be stubborn and selfish, of fixed opinion and dictatorial. They expect the best and often get it.

Everybody has been at a party or gathering when a Leo has swept into the room. Their presence can arouse admiration – or jealousy. The greatest gift they can give is themselves, and they know it. One friend of a Leo whose dominance had become a little too excessive reported: 'I wouldn't say he's conceited, but he's absolutely convinced that if he hadn't been born, people would want to know why not.'

But it doesn't mean that imperial Lions know how to handle money. Far from it. They are used to a plentiful supply and to using it, but not really to managing it.

From infancy, Leos are attracted to valuable things. They will grab at glittering jewellery as their parents lift them from the cot. Throughout their childhood, they will display their flair for drama, acting up to force a bribe from a parent, loving clothes and adornments. They are the most stylish dancers in their youthful group, the stars of the school play, the extravagant, dashing and popular nucleus of their set.

They're always inclined to splash money about liberally, especially on clothes, make up, jewellery, rings and baubles. They love fast cars – preferably old MGs or Morgans – and even if they can't afford a reliable car will make a trendy virtue out of having an old but once-good banger.

They won't ever have to spend on garage bills – there will always be an adoring friend to fix the car for them. They're inclined to take extravagant holidays – Leos are always the ones to show up with a midwinter sun tan (sometimes it's out of a bottle, but don't tell them you know) and love flashy, colourful clothes, especially silks and velvets.

Advertising men love Leos. They can sell Leos anything, if it's colourful, exclusive and expensive. Lions, beware.

The average Leo secretly wouldn't mind being able to be a quieter person sometimes, and those with stronger personalities manage very successfully to become strong silent leaders, but often they feel obliged to show off just a little. They feel they must live up to a larger-than-life role, spending money carelessly and quickly and too often having quietly to beg a loan from a friend.

They don't shop – they take over the store. They don't like to frequent sales because they feel it's somehow shabby not to pay full price. They don't like to use mail order buying either, because they don't have an audience of salespeople to impress.

Some Leos like to be involved in group purchasing schemes, where a dozen friends will band together to buy in bulk. You can tell the Leos when it's time to decide what the cooperative will buy next. The Lions are the ones trying to persuade their friends that buying caviar in bulk is a good idea, while the friends are the ones who simply want to stock up on soap powder.

Leos handle credit well – because they have the confidence to sweep into the credit manager's office and impress him so he will give them more than they can really justify. They like to have a pocketful of credit cards, usually of the gold, special customer variety, and enjoy using them. Curiously they rarely seem to get into deep water with their debts. They think big, spend big and live a larger-than-life role.

When they are owed money, Leos are sometimes apt to dismiss the debt with a grand sweeping gesture – although they usually have the tact not to do it publicly. When they owe money, they are equally likely to dismiss the matter as unimportant – and often convince their creditors it's unimportant, too.

Leos can save money by entertaining at home, by using their special flair to create an illusion to make an ordinary dinner an event. With a few candles, a bottle or three of wine and Leo's stage presence, a dinner party at home can be more enjoyable than an expensive restaurant meal. They can save money from their frequently-large clothing bill by finding a similarly-inclined Leo with whom to exchange clothes. After all, they rarely wear out clothes, they just like to dazzle with their latest acquisition.

They'll never be thrifty, but their likeable natures and ready wits will also ensure that they'll only rarely arrive at the door of the Bankruptcy Court. Leos have lots of friends and enjoy some special protection from them. After all, we need Leos to bring some dash and dazzle, some magic and razzmatazz into our lives – let's save the Lions.

VIRGO (23rd August – 22nd September)
Constant and dutiful, accurate and perfectionist, they are the virgins of the Zodiac. They are not always tolerable, of course. They can be prim, smug and far too easily offended. They can be calculating, unemotional and pedantic. But they can be loving, loyal, diligent, unquestioning, tolerant and wonderfully warm, too. Virgos aren't exactly dynamic fun – they are too straitlaced for that – but in a predictable and loving way they are the sort of people most of us want around most of the time. Show us a shifty Virgo and we'll fall about in confusion. Show us a dishonest Virgo and we'll be dumbfounded.

If we had to choose one word for Virgos that was to summarise their quintessential qualities, we would have to say they are *particular*.

Every aspect of their lives, from their schoolbooks to their account books as adults; from their freshly-pressed blouses for school to their crisply-pleated skirts as businesswomen (or immaculate trousers if they are businessmen, of course) every single aspect is Guardsmanlike perfect. It's their wont, of course. Virgo people just *are* that way.

So you can guess just how the average Virgo reacts when it's time to start handling money. With a personality that's loveable, but with traits that incline the Virgo to precision, accuracy, exactness and diligence you can readily and accurately assume that the average Virgo isn't going to be sloppy in any personal habits, much less with money.

Virgo people have that casual, absolute, unerring knowledge – they are usually right. They rarely need to scratch and scrub at an error on a page. They are deliberate, accurate, careful – and correct. They plan their lives, from puberty onwards, with awesome accuracy. They decide on the type of mate they want, and get exactly that. They choose a career and if they don't exactly light up the world with their incandescence, at least they are exactly where they planned to be just when they planned to be there. Virgos might not be dramatic, on-stage-all-the time people, but they gather real and loyal friends who recognise their valuable talents. They handle people as they handle money – carefully. They are considerate, charming, introverted and faithful.

They prepare carefully considered accounts, balanced exactly to the penny. They enjoy the romance of the elegantly-prepared balance sheet, they all possess purses, be they male or female. At any given moment any Virgo knows, accurately enough, how much is in their possession. Some can even account for compound interest on their deposit accounts.

They are alert, considerate and careful. And there's a major Virgo weakness. They are too careful at times. Come the opportunity when the iron is hot – and the typical Virgo will want to find a thermometer. Money is too important to them to be trifled with.

They are inclined more to the safe 5% return from the local bank than the slightly speculative 10% return from the stock market. Sales and special offers fill Virgoans with fear. Only a Virgo who has been shopping for a specific item for several weeks, who knows exactly what it should cost and who finds it 20% cheaper in a sale will buy it – but only then after he has been assured that he has the right to return it if it's faulty. They are just the same with the special offers, with mail order goods and with anything they can't go and buy at the same price this time next week. If it's got to be bought soon, there must be something wrong – that's the natural Virgo caution at work.

But Virgoans are the banker's favourite customers. They rarely default on a debt, they are meticulous about paying off what they owe. Their very purity of spirit means they feel that a debt is a taint on their lives; their simplicity of purpose means they want to be free to act as they will – and a debt is an unwanted encumbrance, one that is only taken on under necessary circumstances.

Credit cards are a mystery to Virgo people – unless they are sophisticated above the natural levels of this simple, unadorned sign. Why anybody would want to give them free money, even if it is only for a month at a time, is beyond their trusting, uncommercial minds. So they might well obtain a credit card or two, and they might even use it now and then, but generally they will know, accurate to within a few units, exactly what they have outstanding until the end of the month. Immediately the statement arrives, the Virgo is compelled to write a cheque to cover it. Credit is sinful, debt is worse.

For the people who owe Virgoans money, there is one word of advice: pay. Even better: pay quickly. Virgoans hate having money outstanding, and if they paid you the supreme compliment of lending you some, you should retain their respect and friendship by repaying them as quickly as possible.

LIBRA (23rd September – 22nd October)
Librans are scared of handling money, but once they have to do it, they want to know everything about it – and they do it well.

It's just a question of practice. Librans are always reluctant to start things, but once they overcome that initial inertia, they do splendidly. They are logical and intellectual, they love to analyse, they love to be fair, to study every side of an argument or a problem. They are deliberate – but once the decision is made, they know they are in the right. They genuinely try to get things right and proper, and if there's an element of self-deception involved at times, that's just to help the picture become a little more black and white. Librans hate indecision or nuances of meaning.

Librans bring energy to everything they do. They are quietly efficient, they are not lovers of great noise and bustle, they are clean, neat, loving, peaceful and gentle. Natural optimists, they have the wonderful ability to act as peacemakers, and because they are patently fair people love to accept their decisions.

On the negative side, they can be irritatingly indecisive. They love to please, hate making decisions. Ask them what they'd like for dinner and it's 'I'll have what you're having' which is convenient once or twice, but does saddle other members of the Zodiac with someone else's decisions.

Where money is concerned, it's the same. Librans would rather opt out. They love to hand over the cheque book and the month's bills to their spouse, lover or business partner. Usually they will mutter something about them not being any good at this kind of thing and disappear into another room to read or play music, while the unfortunate left with the task agonises over where that missing £10 went.

Yet under that soft interior lurks a mind like a steel trap. Just get Librans involved and watch them go. They aren't lazy or incompetent, just very willing to be self-effacing. It somehow seems fair to them. Their whole life is one of balances and equal shares, and they always enjoy themselves, so feel that usurping the authority of another – taking away their power of cheque book, for example – just isn't fair.

Convince them otherwise, and everyone's happy. For Librans make meticulous book keepers. They have an innate ability to handle money few people suspect. They realise that there is a pattern to it, and their lives are usually made to follow patterns. They see, in broad, wide-angle vision, that financial upsets are temporary, that windfalls are also temporary. They understand that lean years follow fat ones – and they are happy to make financial provision to smooth out the income and outgoings.

Buy the Libran in your life a splendid, imposing account book and watch him set about producing impeccable reckonings. Every penny will be accounted for, every possible record kept. It's a natural inclination. They will make a one, two, ten year plan, become expert on insurances and investments, provide a handsome income for retirement and keep money in sensible ways – and they'll love it. Just convince Librans to handle the family finances and all will be well.

Their only weakness is that they might vacillate a little, pondering the merits of this trust fund against that – but it isn't a major problem.

Librans make wonderful sales shoppers. They scan newspapers for word of upcoming sales, know exactly what they want to buy, go to considerable lengths to find exactly what they want, at the right price; often buy Christmas presents months ahead because they find the perfect gift for a hard-to-please relative and treat shopping as a science rather than something that just happens.

Managing credit also comes easily to most Librans. They know how to apply for it, keep a constant watch on how much is outstanding against which credit card at what time of the month – almost to the point of having envelopes ready stamped and waiting to go the instant the monthly statement drops on the doormat.

Curiously, Librans don't like to use credit cards anyway. They feel they are somehow immoral, if useful, and prefer cash or a carefully filled in cheque. It's just a foible, but that's what happens when you are born under the sign of the scales.

Debts and debtors fill Librans with horror. If a Libran has to owe somebody something, you can be assured that at the first possible moment that debt will be repaid. They have morals, scruples, high standards – and debts just do not sit well with the Libran character.

Similarly, the Libran hates to have somebody in debt to them. It isn't, well, *tidy*. It's an imbalance, something that an organised person doesn't do. Soft-hearted Librans often will lend money, but they don't like doing it, and people who would rather keep Librans as friends won't even ask.

Equally, buying on hire purchase or through the mail. doesn't strike Librans as a good idea. It is convenient, given Libra's occasional spending excesses – they like the odd splurge on something pleasurable, like a shiny new gadget for the house – but it doesn't fit well with their sense of propriety. Librans like things neatly packaged, mentally. They feel that the only real purchase is one where you hand over the cash at the time and walk away with a brown paper parcel under one arm. Anything else isn't quite right.

So, to sum up: Librans have a marvellous capacity to handle money. All they need is a little encouragement to do it. Everyone benefits, because they are talented and meticulous, rarely make careless purchases, because they spend time mulling over the options and they are, in a few words, old fashioned about money and proud of it.

SCORPIO (23rd October – 21st November)
Here's the Zodiac sign that can either be rich beyond the dreams of avarice or poorer than the most undernourished church mouse – Scorpio, ironwilled, determined, impressively impossible when they want to be. They can do anything

they set their minds to, those born under this sign of the Scorpion – and of the Eagle.

Scorpio is ambitious and enterprising if he so chooses. If, however, something sets him against a project, he'll be equally stubborn in opposition, even if it means cutting off his nose to spite his face. Scorpions tend to be secretive and temperamental. They're rebels, they're creative and trustworthy if you make friends with them – but make terrible enemies.

By inclination, they are loyal, because they form very strong attachments very quickly, but it's easy to take a false step and alienate them. They are forceful, emotional and expressive, have penetrating brains, are bold and competitive and like to mentally define their goals before setting out to gain them.

It's a very strong point in Scorpions' favour when they are dealing with financial matters, because they usually know exactly what they want from a deal. No woolly-headed impulse shoppers, these, no suckers for the soft sell or the glittering special offer. No, as in all they do, Scorpions can be calculating. They will coldly and logically decide just what they want, and set about getting it. The problems come when they allow their very strong emotions to intrude – as they invariably do. For Scorpions are among the most sensual of the Zodiac's signs. They have great personal magnetism, often have an air of mystery and sexuality and very quickly acquire a taste for sensual pleasures. That's where they can get into all kinds of financial difficulties. Scorpions might logically know what's the best course to take, but they want to indulge *now*, not in some remote distant future – so they'll go baldheaded for whatever is their present goal.

It isn't exactly impulse dealing, rather an irresistible force which possesses Scorpions so they'll deliberately overspend, knowing full well that the overdraft won't take it but really not caring too much, either. Then, later, passion spent, they'll be full of guilt and remorse and wonder if it was all really worth it – until the next time.

So how to handle it? One Scorpion friend never carries a cheque book or credit cards, reasoning that the pocketful of pound notes which should be sufficient for his daily needs won't really be missed if such a spending frenzy comes over him.

Another depends heavily upon her Taurus husband. She won't shop without him – to his considerable disgust – refuses to have charge accounts at department stores, and keeps a relatively small amount in her personal current account, reasoning that the bother involved in going to the bank to withdraw from her savings account gives her a chance to talk herself out of the impulse purchase she wants to make. She uses another trick, too. She'll 'buy' that beautiful leather coat but not leave the shop with it, instead she'll ask the assistant to put the coat aside for a day until she has had time to see if she can find a matching pair of shoes, or a handbag, or just the right silk scarf. She reasons that by the time she has found the complete wardrobe, she's already overcome her crush on the coat, is sick of shopping and has saved all her money because she never took possession of any of the things she chose.

It really means that those perspicacious Scorpions can view their own weaknesses, decide how best to overcome them – and act.

Financial drive is no problem for Scorpions – they have it aplenty. Planning their lives isn't a real problem: they are clear-sighted enough to know what they are likely to want at any given stage of their lives, and will coolly sit down and make plans for ten or twenty years hence – then not be surprised when they actually carry them out.

It makes long-range financial planning a joy for professionals involved with them – with typical Scorpion efficiency they know what yields to expect, when and how to invest, and how much they need to accumulate to accomplish goals set twenty years in the future.

One weakness is that they rarely stay with one accountant or investment planner for long – they are too secretive. It doesn't make for continuity in their overall money making scheme, but they're more comfortable knowing that there isn't somebody out there who knows all their financial secrets.

When it comes to debts, Scorpions can be shockers. They treat someone who owes them money as an enemy, and consider it a personal insult if their debtor can't cough up the full amount on time. The best rule for Scorpions is: don't lend money to your friends, even for a good reason. That way, Scorpions keep their friends – and the friends keep the Scorpions. If someone asks a Scorpion for money, tell them to go and seek out a Cancerian friend – they'll love to lend out the money.

Creditors: here's one of those odd paradoxes – Scorpions love to have people lend them money and don't mind paying it back, but they also somehow regard being in debt as shameful. They like getting the money because it's a sign of being liked, and they don't mind repaying it because they are trustworthy, but the fact of being indebted to someone intrudes on their ingrown secretiveness. Moral: don't bother borrowing – it's too much grief for the average Scorpion.

A last thought: Scorpions do well at special sales. They are organised enough to make a list of what they want, then take enough money for what they require and not much more. They can withstand the impulse to buy, buy, buy because they can tell themselves: 'Yes, but I need these things on my list.' Then, knowing what they want and what it should cost means they are best equipped to take advantage of sales time.

SAGITTARIUS (22nd November – 21st December)
If any one of all the Zodiac signs needs this book, it's those born under the sign of the Heavenly Archer. For they are detached, spiritual, idealistic and totally impractical by nature. Money just doesn't matter to them. Sagittarians aspire to higher, better things – and usually get there. They

tend to be religious, to be athletic and active, to have a certain duality of character (like their soulmates, Gemini) and are generally optimistic and frank, loyal, open minded and honest.

On the other side of the coin, their impracticality, dogmatism (sometimes even fanaticism) and gullibility make them poor business people. They can be spendthrift, are often gamblers and are inclined to excesses as they follow their restless spirit's inclinations.

But Sagittarians are wonderful friends, cheerful, loyal and open minded. They are clear sighted about future matters, are persevering and generally quite well balanced. If something goes wrong, they're philosophical about it all, have tremendous energy and enthusiasm and work best alone. They hate to have a boss and will rebel if a boss does attempt to lay down the law to them.

They can't handle money, but are cheerfully honest about that minor failing. It just isn't too important to them, and if they have plenty they give it away; if they have little they just shrug and say it wasn't to be.

By their very natures, the patterns of their lives tend to be free flowing. They don't set out rigid plans and stick to them – they take what comes, enjoy it and eagerly wait to see what's next. And that's just about the way they regard their finances. Certainly, the Sagittarian will consider making provisions for the future, but generally that's as far as it goes. Scratch an artist, you'll find an astrological Archer. They are happiest just trusting that their creative abilities will carry them through financial crises. Making money doesn't matter – there will always be somebody to donate a meal.

And, of course, that's true. They trust their instincts and are rarely disappointed. Their inclinations are usually accurate, they want to be detached from hard, practical matters like planning and money. They like to spend money (who doesn't?) but it's usually in small amounts. They like to buy things like new 2B pencils, reams of crisp white paper, tickets for theatre, text books (especially those involving legal matters) and brightly-coloured sweaters.

Sagittarians resist special offers and sales well. They just aren't as materialistic, as determined to save a penny as others of the Zodiac. So the essential bait – something for less than its real value – isn't as tasty. Theirs is one of the signs which needs to have credit cards, not for status or convenience, but simply because it's a good way for whoever organises their financial lives to find out what they are spending, and on what.

Curiously, for such detached, slightly disorganised folk, they are meticulous about keeping accounts straight. They keep monthly bills in one place, and pay them promptly at one time; they keep bank statements tidily together, often even in order; they can produce the year before last's electricity bill and they always have a small stock of postage stamps. That's just the way they are.

Sagittarians believe that long-term financial planning is buying Premium Bonds and hoping. Actually, it isn't such a bad system – they are lucky gamblers, the system makes them feel they're somehow being supportive of the nation and they have crisp, banknote-like certificates to show for their money, not just figures in a bankbook.

They do like to keep a hoard of money somewhere handy, too. Most Archers will have a box or jar full of silver coins – not cupro-nickel, but silver. Some few will even have a collection of sovereigns or other gold coins. It's, well, *tangible*.

Debts and debtors make the Sagittarian reveal himself in his true light. Sagittarians are the Zodiac's philanthropists. Anybody can approach them for a loan, and not only will they generously give anything they can (and sometimes more: one Sagittarian youth in working-class Salford generously donated his parents' garden gate to his church youth club when they needed one) but they will rarely expect it to be returned, unless the debtor has a dramatic change in his fortunes.

As debtors themselves, Sagittarians are at best casual. Money means little to them, and their sense of property isn't too developed. They will gratefully accept a loan, truly meaning to repay it, but when they have scraped the money together are often liable to pass it over to some other needy soul, ignoring their creditor's pleas.

Some Sagittarians live in almost permanent debt, and are cheerfully resigned to the fact. Whatever they put into their bank accounts is likely to fly away to the first person with a sob story – leaving the poor Archers to find money somewhere to pay the grocery bills. We suspect that many Sagittarians don't even know that not everyone is in debt, although if they did know, it wouldn't matter.

If you owe a Sagittarian money – get it to him quickly. He needs it to give to someone else. If he owes you money – beware. And please be understanding. Sagittarians are honest but openhanded, with their own as well as other people's money. One way a business friend of ours knows to retrieve otherwise uncollectable debts from Sagittarians who beseige his art supplies shop is to invite them to repay him with a painting or other craftwork. Then he'll sell it. Everyone is happy – he sells them materials, they have the pleasure of creating something and knowing it will sell and they'll make a small profit while the businessman retrieves the costs of his materials. It isn't very practical and businesslike, but it certainly pleases people.

One last weakness of the Sagittarians: animals. They love pets, will spend far more on them than they will on themselves, and will go to extremes to care for a dependant animal. It's a way to a Sagittarian's heart – to fuss over his or her pet. Better still, buy the pet some food – and help the poor Archer feed himself.

CAPRICORN (22nd December – 19th January)
This is one of the classic Earth signs, symbol of the

astrological Goat, conservative and cautious yet ambitious and responsible, a true Money Sign, with tendencies to be miserly and materialistic, to be rigid and suspicious of others less able. It's a sign of solid worth, of dependability, of prudence and industry, a quintessential sign of the British Victorians.

For Capricorn people are the captains of industry, the moral, duty-bound, practical and efficient movers and shakers whose money-making abilities, given only minimal chances, will dazzle and overpower any opposition.

They can be ruthless and determined, will brook no opposition, are self controlled – except on occasion – and conscientious. They can be a little boring, rather over-whelmingly Calvinistic in their diligence, but they know what they want and they spare neither themselves nor others to get it.

Capricorns are not among the most sympathetic of the Zodiac's twelve signs, nor are they the most creative or imaginative. Their virtue is based on industry. They flog themselves, they are painstaking and intelligent in their attitudes. Their characters come from a similar iron mould – outwardly unyielding, intolerant of others less talented, less willing to work, yet inwardly more humble than anyone would suspect.

They like to make money, not for the material rewards it brings but for the power it confers. We know an American newspaper publisher who is a Capricorn who shows all the stern characteristics of his sign. He is industrious, working seven days a week. He never takes a holiday, never uses his millions to travel or enjoy the luxurious trappings people expect. He drives a modest car and dresses simply. He enjoys a few things: the power his millions and his newspaper give him, his family and the power he has to lavish rewards on his employees. He is a typical Capricorn – seeking power for itself. Money is unimportant to Capricorns once they have sufficient for their simple needs. Money is just a tool. It can be used – and they normally do use it.

Capricorns are generally underrated in the Zodiac. They tend to have subdued personalities, to be too businesslike for most people's taste. They maintain their air of caution, of distance, preferring to be practical and uninvolved. They are money handlers, organisers. They love matters military, martial and mechanical – because these are systems with organisation, and Capricorns love organisation. They will keep their cheque books balanced to the penny, shop with the aid of a calculator – and know exactly what the supermarket checkout bill should be – and keep their desks polished, clear and in geometrical array.

Their lives run like the Swiss railway system – on time, on the rails and like clockwork. By their early teens, Capricorns have mapped out which universities they will attend, what kind of degrees they will obtain, where they will make their mark in the world, and how they will live. Surprisingly, they often carry out every facet, every phase of their grand plans.

It's an interesting aside that most Capricorns marry some diametrically opposed member of the Zodiac, like Gemini, whose flighty, butterfly personality complements their own.

Underneath the Capricorn's outer shell of Teutonic efficiency lies a layer of more efficiency, then a butter-soft sentimental layer, then steel. Touch their sentiment, and they crumble. They wish more people could disregard their austere façade, at least sometimes.

Mail order offers, special sales and the kind of personal bargains that we all come across from time to time – a friend moving and not needing that nearly-new piece of furniture, for example – are all pitches which Capricorns cannot resist. They love bargains, so long as they do not involve too much outlay.

For major purchases, their iron self-discipline means they

are consumer guide shoppers, carefully learning about every possible option before committing a penny. Trust them to know which car, which steam iron or which money market fund offers the best deal, and they will be accurate within a half per cent, every time.

Capricorns are not impulse shoppers. Even their few impulse buys – that piece of unwanted furniture – can and often are resold quickly, at a profit.

They have an inbuilt ability to handle money. Credit cards were not designed for Capricorns. They know about them, use them contemptuously, using the free credit that goes with every card. They pay every credit account on the nail, every month, and save themselves hard cash doing it. They have charge cards of every kind, keep the customer copies in a special place, balance every account every month and are enviably organised.

They know the bank manager by name – and he knows their name, respectfully – they even shopped to find just the right bank and services for them. They always find the lowest mortgage rate, or the cheapest hire purchase agreement (one Capricorn we know was buying a piano, for cash. He found the shop had an incredibly low interest rate on hire purchase, realised he could make a few pounds a year more by leaving his cash in a savings account and bought the piano on HP instead – that's how canny Capricorns can be).

Capricorns have weaknesses. They make poor debtors, worse creditors. They are so businesslike that they hate to be in debt at a personal level. They don't mind taking out mortgage debts on property, or obtaining loans to finance business ventures, but to borrow money for personal purchases seems to them immoral. They resent the debt, and have difficulties paying it off – because it's their subconscious way of protesting 'You shouldn't have lent me the money in the first place. I could have done without it.'

As creditors, they are hardly better. They feel they could be doing something more creative with their money than merely taking the few per cent they will charge even friends and relatives as the price of a loan. Don't bother to borrow from Capricorns – they will only harass you until the loan is repaid, and then they'll feel they were doing you a great favour which should somehow be repaid too.

Capricorns can be selfish, they can be exacting, rigid and even secretive. But they are dependable, honourable, just, faithful and undemonstrative. They can give a lot, expect little in return except the same loyalty they give others and they can be regarded as the Zodiac's equivalent of a computer. Just program them properly and they are yours.

AQUARIUS (20th January – 19th February)
The Aquarian motto is 'I know'. They know just how to give first aid, how many legs on a spider, what is the membership of Lloyds, which streets lead into Ludgate Circus and how many people a day become millionaires. They are amiable walking encyclopedias. Their heads stuffed full of trivia, their lives overflowing with interest, Aquarians are among the most envied of the Zodiac's dozen signs. They are people's people.

They love to study life, are pioneers, constant friends – if sometimes a little hard to contact because of their other friends – are unconventional, retentive, cooperative, intuitive and persistent. Visionaries one and all, they are not particularly materialistic. They are best typified by the hippies of the 1960s, are sometimes criticised for being eccentric or bohemian (it depends on your age which adjective you prefer) and they are both impetuous and rebellious.

Aquarians spark off each other. They need constant stimulus, hence their large circle of friends and interests. Money for them is one small part of life, although it is an interesting one, as it can give them freedom. They are interested in ways to make money, but often lack the diligence to follow through their own ideas, although they are persistent people. It is simply that some things are less interesting than others – and they prefer to persist at following the butterfly that interests them today.

Their wide range of interests and their inherent intelligence usually means that they are knowledgeable people – although they are rarely specialists. Few laser physicists are Aquarians. They are more likely to be found as entrepreneurs, trading in silk today, timber futures tomorrow.

Inventive and progressive, Aquarians love to feel they are part of a larger brotherhood – and they usually are, because they are attractive people whose personalities ensnare almost everyone they meet. It is a useful trait in business, as they can and do use the old boy network to find out what is really happening to their money, or where to buy at the right price.

Aquarians rarely make plans for their lives. They are creatures of the air, and prefer to let the winds of life take them along – but there is often a similar pattern in the way their lives are shaped. In their teens they are rebels, and turn against the materialism of their parents. As young adults, they raise free-spirited children in either visionary or crank ways – depending on how you view Aquarians – and as middle-aged adults they join society 'to change it from within'.

They are loving and loveable, often protected from themselves by their many friends, who recognise that impractical Aquarians neither care about nor adequately can take full advantage of their own talents when it comes to financial planning.

Happily, their friends will do their thinking for them, and offer advice – which is often accepted. Aquarians have the ability but not the inclination to handle money well. They are fountains of ideas, many of them money-making ones.

Aquarians have plenty of money-handling abilities – but they rarely care to exercise them unless something truly interests them. They are able to wander into an auction and buy everything – or nothing. They resist special offers and sales because they simply do not care about making a profit from buying cheaper than normal. Yet there is an inbuilt weakness: if they are in love, they will spend like Croesus just to make their loved one happy.

Aquarians are rarely materialistic. They are perfect credit card customers, because they use the cards as convenience tools. 'They save carrying cash' Aquarian friends tell us when we ask why they like credit cards. They have no idea that the cards are intended to make purchasing – and indebtedness, with its interest rates – easier, to the profit of the credit card companies. Aquarians are on a loftier plane.

That is a reason why they do not handle money well, because they have no properly-developed sense of values, of property. Money is something which is there, which will always be there, which is a renewable asset. They have no ethic of having to earn every penny, scraping and pinching to make ends meet. And, irritatingly for the rest of us, Aquarians rarely have to. They have a genius for attracting a plentiful flow of cash. They have a natural optimism, an occult trait that is almost magic of attracting money just when they need it.

It means that they are casual about debts, whether to others, or from others. Money to many Aquarians is something that is useful but not an end in itself. Interest for an Aquarian means something he can think about, not a percentage in the bank. Cash flow is something Aquarians have heard about – they read and absorb such a lot – but it isn't something they ever spend time considering. If there isn't enough in the bank account today, there will be tomorrow, they reason.

It is a weakness, but it is a civilised one at least. Unless, that is, an Aquarian owes you money ...

If that is the case, try the approach that few Aquarians can resist: tell them you need the money soon for a creative venture involving people. Be vague – let the Aquarian imagination take over. They'll suggest what your venture should be – and perhaps you will even make money from it!

PISCES (20th February – 20th March)

We hate to say it, but Ebenezer Scrooge was probably a Pisces. He had all the Piscean vices: he was secretive, selfish, reclusive, materialistic. And he had all the same Piscean virtues: he was emotional, receptive, spiritual and philanthropic. It just depends which button gets pressed.

Pisces is a business sign. Pisces people *believe*. They believe in themselves, they can be taught to believe in others. They absorb knowledge, they are responsive and sensitive. And they can make others believe in them. For the last 2000 years we have been in the Age of Pisces – of people dying for their beliefs. The very sign of Christianity was the fish, an interesting linkage of symbols between Christianity and paganism.

Pisceans are idealistic and imaginative – and make good martyrs. They can often create sorrow and unhappiness for themselves and are sometimes accused of making their personal relationships difficult because they enjoy wallowing in misery. They love to cry, will sob their way happily through sentimental movies but are sympathetic to the sufferings of others. They are generally not aggressive, are wonderful story tellers, are adaptable and often self-sacrificing. Pisceans can be hypersensitive and moody, however, and although they are usually intelligent and learn quickly, they are often discontented with themselves and develop totally unjustified inferiority complexes.

They don't really like to handle money in large sums, although they are happy with small amounts because they don't feel that there is any real responsibility attached to modest sums. Many Pisceans would honestly prefer not to have anything to do with money, usually because they have had one or two bad experiences with it as children and feel they are somehow 'unworthy' (a favourite Piscean word) to handle it.

If Pisceans buy gifts, they need to be reassured that the recipients are totally satisfied with them, that the colour is right and so on.

They have certain weaknesses when money does come their way, too. Wealthy Pisceans love to splurge on larger and more expensive cars than they really need – as a way of boosting their often-fragile egos. They won't spend much on their homes, preferring to stay put in a familiar area even if they don't really like it and can afford to move to a better one.

They make excellent aides – as right hand man to a top executive, or as a super-efficient personal secretary, but tend to lack the aggression and confidence to go out and do the boss job themselves. That can put a ceiling on Pisceans' ability to earn the kind of money they often deserve.

When it comes to buying goods, they make excellent sales shoppers, because they love to compare, know exactly what anything is worth, know if it's a bargain and usually know accurately enough what's in their purses or wallets.

Credit cards and Pisceans are uneasy bedfellows. The astrological Fishes think of credit as somehow immoral, and the thought of using 'loans' in the form of unpaid bills is abhorrent to them. They'd rather pay cash. Until, that is, one day an admired friend casually lets them know how convenient credit can be – and then impressionable Pisceans are likely to go out and get a whole pocketful of plastic, which they will use with glee.

They spend money on charities, giving generously to door to door appeals. They plan carefully for retirement and spend on insurances, independent retirement accounts and long-term investments.

Pisceans are scrupulous about debts, rarely incurring personal debts of their own but being generous to a fault about lending money to relatives or friends in need. And, although borrowing isn't something that's quite right for them, it's fine for them to lend others money, they feel. It's an extension of giving to the poor. The Good Samaritan was probably Piscean – that's the sort of philanthropist Pisces is.

The kind of things Pisceans like to purchase might give a clue to their values. They'll buy a good camera and a good car, reasoning that each will last. They love fine furniture but tend to buy 'fashionable' rather than classically simple pieces, so their homes often look a little old-fashioned.

They rarely like to use hire purchase, preferring to save cash until they have the whole amount. Pisceans spend money on travel, know little wrinkles like always changing traveller's cheques at banks when they are away, because they will obtain a better exchange rate than they would at the convenient front desk of their hotels.

Another major area of expenditure is medical expenses. Pisceans have a close affinity to hospitals, they often like to work in and around them, either as medical or auxiliary staff or on fund-raising committees and the like. So it's natural for them to ensure that whenever they or their loved ones go to hospital they go first class, paying for private treatment with the best specialists and sometimes overspending. It's not really an indulgence, it's just the way Pisceans are, and anyway they usually have comprehensive insurance coverage that takes the immediate sting of the cost away from them.

If Pisceans could try to see themselves as Ebenezer Scrooge – and apply a little of the Christmas spirit, as he did – they would find their lives so much better they'd wonder why it didn't all happen before. After all, if Scrooge could reform, so can they.

Chapter Two
Where the money goes

*'Never ask a question to which you really don't want to
know the answer.'*

Dallas Brozik

Most of us tend to think of budgeting as an activity worthy of
the rarefied atmosphere of the boardroom and the bank.
However, it can be easy. Just follow these simple guidelines,
know yourself and thank us kindly.

The basic rules can be understood by anyone capable of
reading. You simply determine what your income is, what
your outgoings are and which of the latter are real priorities or
necessities.

These rules are basic to the whole Zodiac, be they Leos or
Taureans. Make a solemn vow to read them carefully, write
them down – then put what you know into practice. After you
have read the general principles, look up your own section of
the chapter to bring your own, personal astrological traits
into finer focus.

I: calculate your annual income. Take a sheet of paper and
log every item of income you can reasonably expect during
the coming year. It's wise not to be too optimistic – it's better
to have a surplus of income than of outgoings!

II: bring the annual figures down to a manageable amount
by converting them into monthly figures. Remember that
your annual income will include not just your take-home pay,
but also income from investments, bonuses, commissions,

cash gifts from relatives, refunds from the Inland Revenue, debts, profits on anything you might sell and any of the items you know by experience will come to you in the next year.

Employed people should only list their after-tax, take-home income. Remember that you'll have union dues, PAYE deductions, NHI, company pension plan payments, life insurance or company savings plan deductions to come out of that gross figure.

Self-employed people whose income might be a little more irregular should divide the annual total by 12, or perhaps estimate only for one fiscal quarter, and divide that figure into a monthly amount.

Now you have taken the first major step (and probably the hardest) to financial liberation. You know what your real income is, by the month.

III: make a list of necessities – the things you MUST spend money on to stay fed, warm and sheltered. You will have some large annual expenditures – insurances, taxes, especially rates and perhaps even a debt or two. These are not the once-a-month type of spending, but rather a category of once or several times a year spending which must be planned for. List them first. Convert them to a monthly basis, so the £360 rates bill becomes a £30 a month item.

Now list your regular monthly bills. Here's a handy checklist of obvious ones:
* mortgage or rent payments, rates.
* utilities payments – gas, water, electricity, TV rental, telephones, etc.
* instalment payments – hire purchase debts, Christmas Club, credit card payments, personal loans or overdraft repayments.
* medical expenses – drugs, private care bills, dental expenses.
* car running expenses, transportation costs – train, bus

fares, parking bills, average petrol and oil bills, maintenance bills.

* dues and fees to organisations – clubs, unions, charities, professional groups.

* taxes which have not been withheld under PAYE.

* clothing, personal allowances – do you pay for lunches, for example?

Total your unavoidable monthly bills. Now you know both your monthly income and what is your unavoidable monthly outgoing total. The difference will determine much of your lifestyle.

Many experts suggest that you include an amount equivalent to 5% of your monthly income for savings; that you should build up a reserve amounting to two months worth of net income as a financial cushion. If you agree, and it is a sensible plan, add in that 5% to the unavoidable monthly bills category. Now prepare for the next step.

IV: Budget your everyday expenses.

This means you are about to begin robbing Peter to pay Paul. It's the most fascinating insight into each Zodiac sign's secret character because this is where personality comes into play. What is important to one sign is totally irrelevant to another. If you can carry your money management to this point, you will be able to enjoy the luxury of indulging your whims because you have everything on a sound footing.

Take a look at the kind of things that make up the everyday expense category:

* food – grocery bills, restaurant costs, pub snacks, drinks, pet foods, personal items like cosmetics and toothpaste, tobacco and whatever comes out of the office vending machine.

* home services – repairs and renovations, cleaning ladies and materials, lawn care, home improvements.

* transport – anything not listed under essential transportation.

* clothing – dry cleaning and laundry bills, junk jewellery, frills.
* household furnishings – soft furnishings and china, silver and stereos. You'll know.
* personal – haircuts and coiffures, beauty treatments and health clubs. Again, you'll know. Just list everything not already listed.
* sundries – medical expenses not previously listed, pleasure – theatre tickets and magazine subscriptions, holiday expenses, home entertainment, anything else you can think of.

There is one other, tricky factor to add – inflation. Certain parts of the country experience higher inflation than others. Big cities tend to see costs rise quicker than small villages do. Find out what is your own local rate of inflation and try and relate it to your expenditure. Between January 1979 and January 1980 home prices went up some 16% for example. Clothing and its care cost 6.4% more. Yet the average family spent 5.1% of its income on clothing; 45% on housing. All you can realistically do is monitor your major outgoings and see how inflation affects them – then adjust your budget accordingly.

So there it is, the master plan. Just a few rules:
* calculate your annual income.
* convert the figures into monthly ones.
* list necessities to find what's left for daily living.
* list your daily expenses and expenditures to determine priorities.
* remember inflation's effects.

Now, here's what this chapter is all about: how does each sign decide its priorities? You know what you have, what you must put aside. You also know from your list what kind of thing you also spend money on. Some great lights have dawned

– you're beginning to understand why, despite your huge salary, you could never seem to keep up with the Joneses.

Now, faced with the cold, hard figures on your piece of paper, you are clearly seeing what economic assets you have, and what are the possible daily drains on those assets. You are about to begin to plan, to make reasoned choices.

ARIES (21st March – 19th April)
You love cars and spend endlessly on yours. It's a chrome and leather monster that you love dearly – or it's a battered banger that no self-respecting car thief would pinch, but it's yours and you love it.

So a priority on your optional spending is obviously going to be transportation – and that doesn't mean bus fares. You'll be happiest if you splurge on a racy, shiny auto that everyone will envy. Or, if you have that streak of inverted snobbery that's an Arien trait you'll have the battered version of your personal chariot that many will secretly envy too. That's because they wish they also had the self-assuredness to drive about in something held together with knitting wool and exhaust bandage.

You won't miss gourmet meals, you'll live happily on baked beans and toast. You won't regret not having flashy jewellery, genuine mink and the latest hairstyle. You will feel a need for a travelling holiday – and that will admirably fit with your love of your car, because it's just a question of hey-ho for the Channel ferry and off across the Continent for you. It will be a dual pleasure – Ariens love the sense of movement; they also love their cars, so you will combine the two in one ecstatic way.

A possible saving for non-mechanical Ariens is to seek out the small local garage and strike up a personal relationship with the owner. He will usually service your car to the standards you require without you having to take out a second mortgage to pay for its repairs.

Another area of savings since you love to travel and you love the outdoors – make this year's summer holiday a camping one. You'll be delighted to find just how much you can save, and how you can enhance your sense of freedom and independence under canvas. Some Ariens prefer not to rough it too much and instead choose to take a caravan holiday abroad. Check the cost of renting a caravan – you'll save all that capital, reduce maintenance costs on your car because it won't be dragging a caravan around, and you won't have it cluttering up your driveway all year.

Some few words about Ariens when you come to create your own personal money-managing budget: you are resourceful, aggressive and assertive. Don't be carried away on a floodtide of your own optimism about the oncoming year's earnings. Even Ariens can come unstuck.

You are also impulsive so don't try to dash off your budget in ten minutes. It is a basic plan you will use for decades if you plan it carefully. Do it in bursts if you must, but have a cool-headed, methodical friend check it for you to make sure there are no major omissions, or at least survey it yourself several times.

Another thought: you of all the signs are the least likely to plan for retirement or to set aside an emergency fund. Why should you? You have always managed on your wits, even if your financial affairs have been largely a case of feast or famine.

So set aside the modest 5% of your monthly earnings (after taxes and deductions, remember) as a savings account. It isn't the dazzling coup that will give you financial security, but the plodding, methodical widow's mite in the savings bank that will ensure your ultimate comfort and security. For most Ariens, we'd suggest either a standing order or a similar arrangement with your employer to help you save at source.

You Ariens can be headstrong, overbearing and sometimes foolhardy. So remember these traits and plan to defeat them. Why waste such a talent as yours on the unnecessary bother of worrying about money? Make a plan – you are decisive, after all – then implement it in the only way you can. Plan to make yourself independent. It's a major appeal to all Ariens – and it will work.

One last thought, you are highly intuitive so set aside a very small amount of your savings money for a Stock Market flutter each month and watch your savings, and your independence, grow.

TAURUS (20th April – 21st May)

Here's the sign of the Zodiac's banker. You will consistently handle money well, if a little cautiously. You respect it, you enjoy it, you know about it. What priorities do you have in budgeting? Well, Taurus has some weaknesses, including hedonism. There isn't anything wrong with enjoying enjoyment – Taureans are fond of saying that the only thing they can't withstand is temptation – but you do have to provide for it.

Curiously for a sign so cautious, there sometimes emerges in the occasional Taurean a streak of the gambler, a daredevil chancer who will be overtaken by the need to throw off his natural constraints and live on the edge for a while. Well, Taurus, life in the fast lane isn't for you. Ignore those murmuring voices, think instead of the pure pleasure you can obtain from what you have, instead of what you might possibly have but probably won't.

You have vast artistic talent. Call on these skills to cut costs by doing your own interior designing, by painting your home, by making things for it. Even if you have never tried, you'll be surprised at the high quality of the results. Discover your own hidden potential – and save some money.

You need not feel ashamed to set aside a reasonably large slice of your monthly budget for matters relating to art. It might be for tickets to the ballet or theatre. It may be expenditure on art materials, such as brushes and paper or fabrics for making cushions, or wood for putting up cabinets, Taureans can make works of art, however humble, from anything to which they turn a hand. And those skills can make a superb hedge against inflation for Taureans. As you love to do work on your home, remember too that what makes you happy as you do it is also adding valuable equity. You are adding to the value of your home even as you live there because you tend to improve it constantly.

You like fine things, you enjoy the sensual feel of crisp napkins in restaurants, the tinkle of crystal and the clash of silverware. You are reluctant to give up these simple but expensive pleasures, but there is only so much room in the budget for this kind of expense. Something has to go.

Organised Taureans belong to one of the few signs who can make use of a strategy we call the switch plan. Instead of buying brand-name goods, buy generic ones. Instead of pouring the best malt into your guests' mixed drinks (where they won't be able to taste the difference anyway), use a cheaper brand of blended Scotch. Instead of always buying the tastiest cuts of beef for a casserole, buy cheaper ones and use a slow cooker to enhance the flavour. Instead of sending everything to be dry cleaned, slowly replace your wardrobe with clothes that only need machine washing. You are not usually car-proud so buy second hand vehicles on which the depreciation bite has been lessened. Take care of your own garden, instead of having a local teenager do it (you usually could do with the exercise, anyway). Instead of popping out to the businessman's restaurant or pub for a snack take a packed lunch to work.

Generally, only Taureans can be self-disciplined enough and know enough about their remarkably stable habits to make this work. You see, to know yourself is half the battle. It's a question of identifying your enemy – and that for Taureans is knowing that they like to spend on food, on good clothes and on their homes. There is nothing wrong with any of that – but these are things which take cash, and something usually has to give. For Taureans who know their priorities, there will always be something which can give. Everyday expenses are elastic and knowing that can be a great strength.

One last area of the budget on which Taureans tend to overspend is in clubs and associations. You love to join, to be a member of groups. Usually you quickly rise through the ranks to become an officer of the club – and because of the demands of those positions you neglect the other clubs of which you are a member. Simply look at the list, and decide which you really do want to remain with – it could save enough for a gourmet meal for two!

GEMINI (22nd May – 20th June)
Resourceful Geminis are one of the few Zodiac signs capable of making their financial lives operate smoothly without a budget – but if you have one it can help. As the dual personality people of the stars, Geminis are equally attracted to the thoughts of either having a freewheeling financial life – or of being terribly organised. The trouble is, your attitudes tend to change with the weather.

The best thing for Geminis to do is to follow the instructions on how to set up a budget, but not to feel that you have to be too rigid in applying those rules to yourselves. That way you can have your cake and eat it – and as you'll know what you should be doing, at least some of the advice will be helpful.

Geminis tend to think of books, theatre, off-beat entertainments (such as parachuting or shark fishing) as more important than setting up a savings account, and with their ability to fall cat-like on their feet, who is able to argue with them?

One successful piece of advice Geminis have so far always enjoyed is when we tell them they are all cyclists at heart. Most go out and borrow or buy a bicycle just to find out, and the sense of travel, of wind in the hair and of honest effort suits them down to the tyres. The fact that riding a bicycle helps save petrol, invigorates them and also adds some extra lustre to their image as slightly eccentric is also delightful.

Another budget-saving hint which especially applies to Geminis is that the local library has shelves full of books to be read – and all for free.

For savings, it helps to set up special accounts for planned adventures, be it a trip to Morocco, a week at a rock climbing school or a special cruise in the Caribbean. The savings accounts by themselves are uninteresting to Geminis – so ask your friendly local banker if you can open an account actually labelled 'Jamaican Getaway' to encourage you to keep making deposits. Geminis we know who have done just this take an especial delight in showing their friends their labelled passbooks and telling them what sacrifices they have had to make for that travel dream still unfulfilled.

Curiously enough, Geminis do make good professional accountants because they are so efficient if they set their minds to it. They aren't the dry-as-dust variety, though. More likely you'll find they are the kind with dashing cars, outrageous ties and a pocketful of sweets for any passing child. There's a strong strain of theatre in Gemini, they love to know what's going on, to communicate, gossip and discuss. They will watch television avidly and read everything from the tide tables in the morning paper to the international telephone codes in the directory. Geminis are suckers for expensive radios, fine stereos and electronic gadgetry. Yet, having bought a new toy, they'll often give it away, impulsively. Try to read the consumer guides before you buy anything. Visit the library and do the research you do so well, to find out just what is the best buy. By the time you get around to actually buying it, you'll be tired of the idea anyway, and if you didn't really need it, then there's a saving, because you'd only have given it away later.

Two things that most Geminis would have and keep are watches and typewriters. So buy good ones because you'll enjoy them both. Clothes are not too important in your scheme of things because you swap and change so frequently. Instead, buy some brightly coloured scarves or accessories which you can mix and match to give your outfits a fresh new look.

CANCER (21st June – 22nd July)
Moon Children, you have probably read the opening part of this chapter, digested just how to make a budget (you probably have a pencil and paper out already, with some rough estimates scratched out on it) and now you have flicked through the preceding pages wallowing in guilt. You don't see how you and a budget can possibly live together. You get a sick feeling when you pick up your mail each day, because you know there is some unpaid bill in it, and frankly you enjoy the worry of it all. Well, a budget *is* for you, none better. And you are for a budget – because you can feel guilty about not keeping to it, just as you don't usually keep to those diets you keep starting.

But your personal economies are usually sound. For you have spent a lot of time ploughing effort and scraped-together savings into your home. And it has appreciated in ways you never suspect. You are probably quite well-to-do, but that isn't enough. For you, your budget has to be aimed at one thing: security.

Everything else is secondary to your peace of mind. You must have an emotional blanket to cuddle under, a sheaf of insurance policies that cover every eventuality. You do it all for the best motives – for your family. You are the original homebody, the loyal, devoted, home-loving Crab. So plan your budget accordingly.

Some Crabs we know have objected to our advice and said, in effect: 'But I already know, fairly accurately, how much money I have and what I have to spend it on.' Yes, yes, we say – but security for you is to sit down and make a budget. That way you have the knowledge that you haven't hidden anything from yourself (Crabs are a trifle secretive), and you can work on the assumption that you have assessed your financial health in stark black and white. Our friends have invariably gone away muttering, only to return a week or so later beaming uncharacteristically and congratulating themselves on being so smart as to draw up their personal balance sheets and money management schemes.

So what to spend it on for best results? Insurances, domestic spending of all kinds, a vacation – Cancerians love holidays, especially in warm water places such as the Mediterranean, Caribbean or the Gulf of Mexico.

Cancerians also tend to spend on good quality things, and would rather have an old but high quality item than a new and cheaper one. Cars are low on the list of priorities because Cancerians tend to keep theirs for a long time. They make long-term purchases, things that might cost more but will last longer, because they form an attachment to their possessions and love to keep them.

Food is another item important on the Cancerian's budget. You love to eat, to entertain. You are proud of your home, and justifiably so. It means that you invite friends home, and as you make such good hosts, they are always angling for invitations. So a lot of your enjoyment can come from dinner parties, from casual evenings with friends and just plain entertaining. Equally, food away from home will make up an important segment of your budget so be prepared to allow for it. Don't forget to count in pub grub, drinks, liquor bills, and the odds and ends like packets of mints from the newsagent's shop when you pick up magazines.

Household furnishings are not a frequent item so tend to be overlooked, but they can be a major expense for Cancerians, as you love to buy the best for your home – sometimes on hire purchase (although you prefer not to, as your home is something you like to look around and say 'All this is mine'.) Happy budgeting, Cancerians, you'll love it.

LEO (23rd July – 22nd August)

Confident, outspoken, generous Leo – you once had a budget, but it was scribbled on a sheet of hotel stationery and you left it somewhere. It didn't matter about losing it because you never had any intention of ever making your life conform to a discipline, anyway. You are accustomed to having your royal whims financially supported and the very thought of having to make financial plans goes against the grain. But you really should try it – you will find that instead of being hampered by a budget, you'll actually be helped by it. Leos are often generous to a fault and a budget will help you understand just where all that money does go. You'll find that an awesome total goes on entertaining others, on gifts and donations that sometimes you frankly cannot afford to make.

Your spending priorities are many and changeable. You enjoy having a splendid car, a splendid home – not for you the cottage with roses around the door, but a real mansion. If you can't have these things, though, you'll simply shrug and say 'Oh, well' and forget them for the time being. So they can't be major priorities.

Your real weakness is clothing. You love fine clothes, and all that goes with them – the accessories, the jewellery, the opportunities to show off not the clothes but yourself in them. So don't feel bad about spending far more on clothes than almost anybody you know. The effect on your morale will be so good you'll be an even better person. You love gold, and as it isn't such a bad investment these days, why not buy some? Besides you can wear it as jewellery and everybody will know how rich and powerful you are – often attracting business offers you wouldn't otherwise have, and turning the image into reality.

Your budget will take account of your regular monthly bills – those boring old things like utility payments and credit card debts and give you a rare clear overview of where the rest goes and allow you to take command of your financial state.

Try to reduce your dry cleaning and laundry bills a little – you'll note that they are often quite high; save slightly on the number of times you visit the beautician or hairdresser because often you'll do it to boost your morale rather than because you truly need to go. Use your undoubted skills to make some home repairs yourself, instead of calling on expensive and often unreliable service people to do minor jobs.

Consider just how much you are spending on food away from home and see if there isn't a practical saving you can make there. You don't need to buy restaurant meals every day, surely? It might suit your image of yourself as a noble leader and someone important, but it doesn't help when you are scratching around to raise a little money for something you really want to do.

And what, after clothes, is your favourite way of spending money? It's on anything to do with the theatre. Partly because you have strong dramatic tendencies yourself and the colour, glamour and bustle of it all appeal so much and partly because it's a great chance for you to show yourself off, too. But why not save some money by joining a local theatre group instead of simply sitting out there in the stalls? Or perhaps volunteer to .help teach small children (some Leos make very fine attention-getting teachers). These and similar limelight-attracting actions will gratify you and serve a useful, money-saving purpose.

Another area in which you can save is transportation in and around cities. You are the types who will jump in a taxi cab at the slightest excuse. Consider using your feet, or the Tube or the bus service. You'll save, and you'll get a secret kick out of how much you save. Another budget-saver for Leos is to buy second-hand jewellery, at flea markets or junk shops. With your eye for adornments, you'll find some excellent bargains and satisfy your passion at the same time. Check, too, on the magazine and newspaper subscriptions you take – how many do you buy because it seemed like a good idea back when ...

You could cancel a few and take yourself out for a splendid meal on the proceeds.

Good luck with your budget efforts, Leos. You are one of the Zodiac signs who could most use a little financial organisation. Think of it as taking command of your own purse strings, as being your own Chancellor – and it will work for you.

VIRGO (23rd August – 22nd September)
You're a member of the Zodiac whose practical nature means you have already taken out a pencil and notepad and halfway drafted a fiscal plan for the coming year.

Virgoans make splendid administrators, accountants and executives. It's one of your natural talents. You love to analyse, dissect and consider. You are meticulous and you'll want to be accurate to the last penny. Try not to be – it's difficult to foresee every single item of income for the coming year and even more difficult to predict outgoings accurately.

Your list of necessities will be thorough, more so than almost any other member of the Zodiac. You will be able to determine what are priorities, what are luxuries, what semi-luxuries are valuable to you in a very cool, honest and economical way. But don't you just long for some small whim now and then?

Here is a secret few Virgoans admit to each other: almost all of you have a little store of what Americans call 'mad money' – cash to be spent on total luxuries, on madcap adventures, on useless, hedonistic goods you would never dream of purchasing out of the housekeeping. So budget a small amount each month for this secret, sinful fund – you'll love to know it's there, will spend hours daydreaming about how you'll spend it and gain far more pleasure from your secret than the money could ever buy. You'll probably get a double boost from this – because almost all Virgos with these hidden funds use them to buy something for someone else! That's a measure of how unselfish you are, and how loving and giving you are, too.

Let's look at a few practical ways to reduce the budget expenditure. It isn't easy, because Virgo is a practical sign not given to lavish spending. However, there are some areas. One is to take a hard look at your stationery and postage costs. You tend to overspend on stationery, and because hou have it you want to use it. So you send long letters to friends. Use lightweight airmail letters for overseas mail – the difference in cost can be startling.

Use your practical talents in other ways, too You are talented at craftwork – consider remaking out-of-style clothing, doing carpentry for use around the house, taking up pottery or painting classes with a view to marketing your products later. Use left-overs and your imagination to produce appetising snacks (a good cook book is a worthwhile investment, too) and allow that imagination of yours to dictate money-saving ways to recycle unwanted toys or household goods.

You can do well by taking a look at household running expenses because, with your discriminating eye, you will see ways to save energy and cost by careful insulation. For you, mechanical things are no mystery, so many Virgoans like to maintain their own cars, service central heating or household appliances themselves and generally do the work of a handyman. Consider putting a slice of your budget down for tools and equipment – after all, they say a workman is only as good as his tools.

Holidays are important to you, so budget for them in plenty of time. Consider taking a holiday with a theme – to visit all the museums in London, for example, or all the art galleries in Amsterdam. You are a formidable tourist, and travel armed with guidebooks, notebooks, sensible shoes and a thirst to soak up everything you can. Holidays spent lying on a beach are not generally for Virgos – they prefer to be up, about and active in their free time.

Allow plenty of room in your budget for medical expenses. You don't like to be caught out, and a good contingency plan will ease your mind more than the modest monthly cost of maintaining it. Similarly, you are inclined to budget against underpayment of taxes, keeping a reserve aside just in case. Use this money as a rainy day savings account, perhaps investing it in short-term money market loans. You'll find that even small amounts put aside quickly become large ones.

LIBRA (23rd September –22nd October)
Gentle, artistic Librans can see an attraction in making a budget – it is something they understand because – in theory – it balances. Librarians are best at seeing both sides of an argument, at carefully considering all the options. But then, fair-minded Librans, you tend to be a trifle indecisive. You can't always choose which priority should oust another. It can be a choice for you between winter boots or winter sports equipment and you will remain undecided until Spring, when the agony of choosing begins all over again.

Probably the simplest thing you can do is work out your budget guidelines, determine just how much you have available for the optional purchases, list them, then find a sensible, practical, down-to-earth friend (you all have them – you'd never get anything done without one), and ask for some advice. Using some other, less cautious friend will at least mean you buy your winter clothes on time. They might not be what you really wanted to buy, but then ...

You are at your best when you come to making purchases for others. A Libran with a family to provide for is a happy one indeed. For you Librans are unselfish and clear-sighted about others. You are idealistic, but you can be practical. You will consider the options before buying a family refrigerator or washing machine, and you will make the exact purchase you should, having first considered all the facts carefully.

So who would guess that you Librans are secretly terrified
of money? You hate the stuff – it carries with it the odour of
responsibility and decision making. Once you are persuaded
to take over and are convinced the responsibility is yours and
nobody minds, all's fine.

Unexpected things get priority in your personal money
management scheme: things like picture framing and art
supplies; sculptures and antique silver. You probably have an
antique silver button-hook collection, or a dazzlingly-
polished selection of old brass and copper on display.
They are among your priorities – so budget for spending on
them.

Because you are a good money manager when you get
under way, your household running costs are generally
lower than your neighbour's. You have an efficient home, you
make the money in your bank account stretch further and you
share a trait with Virgo in that you like to squirrel away small
sums of cash, just in case you want to go out and splurge on
something.

You are a good saver – you understand that small sums
quickly mount up, but you prefer the sock under the bed to the
savings account at the local bank. Consider the more
organised way and your money will grow quicker.

You might also budget for a small monthly investment
account. You have the self-discipline to set aside regular
sums, so why not put a small amount aside each month for
speculation with a local stockbroker? It's more reliable than
money in a sock, in that it should increase, it has the added
bonus of adding a certain spice of chance to your savings and
it can be retrieved if you need to cash it in.

Here are some items you might have overlooked in
your budget – you like flowers and flower arrangements, so
plan for buying supplies; you enjoy artistic things, and
will give time and money to support cultural activities,
so budget for that, too. You will want to attend concerts, to
have your children take music lessons, so there is another

item; you prefer not to tinker with mechanical things, so allow a little more for car or household appliance services. You enjoy travel, and as you are prepared to do it cheaply your annual holiday need not cripple you for the year. Consider a barge or sailing holiday, especially through the European canals and river systems where both your peaceful nature and your artistic eye will be delighted.

One simple way to make establishing a budget and then sticking to it attractive to you is to prepare a graph of what savings you can expect and when, in the coming year. If you break the graph down into savings on fixed, optional and future expenditures your analytical mind will be delighted, your progress will be more interesting and you'll positively enjoy the savings you make – before you actually reward yourself by spending them.

SCORPIO (23rd October – 21st November)

Scorpions and a budget can be either a marriage made in heaven or an accountant's nightmare. It's either something you Scorpions pursue with all the energy and persistence at your command, or it's something you struggle to avoid.

Scorpio's tenacity can mean considerable savings because you have the ability to seek out the bargains you want, make the deals you wish for, and to shape your financial life just exactly the way you would like.

But first you Scorpions have to decide, for yourselves, not as a sop to someone you love, that this is indeed the course you wish to follow.

Your priorities in a budget are fairly straightforward – you will use that Eagle logic to provide a sensible financial masterplan to provide for yourself and your loved ones, you'll use your organisational flair to maintain the plan as you go along. A problem area for you is an appeal to your emotions. If a clever salesman can persuade you that you can't live without a new car or a microwave oven then you are lost. And you can hardly budget for it, either.

One possible way to control the emotional impulse is to establish a separate savings account to be used purely for major purchases. What are the kinds of things you Scorpios will want, on impulsive and emotional grounds? Just about any luxury consumer good – from a home computer to a kitchen gadget. As a child you will have saved every coin to buy a bicycle or skateboard or leather football – because you wanted it. As an adult, those same impulses will motivate you. You'll splash out on a luxury cruise or a home extension. Book club subscriptions and bunches of roses, new clothes and old silver, oak dining room tables, Waterford crystal, Irish linen, Cuban cigars – anything that hints of quality and expense will lure you to spend.

You'll also spend money recklessly to help others, often for things they really don't need. One Scorpion friend 'loaned', without much hope of ever seeing it returned, almost all her savings so a friend could take a 'restful' holiday in Greece. 'She seemed to need it' explained the friend, who really needed the holiday more herself. But it was a typical grand gesture by the high-flying Eagle.

On a practical note, you Scorpions should ensure that your monthly outgoings are properly covered, see that your insurances are up to date and your major debts – mortgage, hire purchase, credit cards – are provided for before you go window shopping. Try to shop with a shopping list, to reduce the tug on your impulses. Read consumer guides and talk to friends before you go out to do battle with salesmen for a major purchase, and allow yourself a cooling-off period before you finally commit yourself to a big outlay. You'll be surprised how many of these 'must-have' purchases seem less attractive the morning after.

You know you have strong emotions – but you also have equally strong self discipline. Play the one off against the other – and you'll be a wiser and wealthier Eagle.

SAGITTARIUS (22nd November – 21st December)
For the Sagittarian, a budget isn't an option – it's a necessity.
You who are born under the sign of the heavenly Archer just
aren't in tune with the nasty everyday practicalities of
handling money – so you rarely seem to have any. It slips away
like fine sand through an hourglass – steadily but inevitably.
With a budget, you will only have a portion of your income
directly within your generous, open hands – so your financial
ratings will improve dramatically, with the attendant benefit
of added peace of mind.

You Sagittarians are optimistic, intelligent, creative, loyal,
cheerful and tolerant. You need all these excellent qualities
because you find unexpected financial difficulties in your life
that really shouldn't be there. You make enough money to live
comfortably, but there always seems to be yet another bill.
Well, as the snake oil salesman said, here's the answer. Make a
budget. Follow the instructions earlier in this chapter, setting
aside money to cover the essentials and you'll find you have
your optional spendings left over. Whatever you do with
them, you can't do serious damage to your financial health.
You might find you're a bit short of food in the refrigerator
one day, or that the car really does need a tune-up, but you
won't have hordes of creditors banging at your door because
you forgot to pay the bills.

What is the typical Sagittarian's weak spot, his likeliest
route to the depths of financial problems? Sagittarians have a
fondness for games of chance, for gambling. You would
rather speculate on the progress of two raindrops down a
window pane than eat a meal. And often that's the way of it.
Far be it from us to deter you from your weakness. We just
want you to know about it – because then you can help
yourself. All we'd like is that you chance only amounts you
can afford to lose. Write 'gambling' into your list of budget
items. After all, it is one of your priorities. Whether it's
worthwhile is another matter – but if you recognise it, you can
defeat it.

You're the Peter Pans of the Zodiac, carefree (at least outwardly – sometimes you hide your inner woes and worries, for the best reasons) and always youthful. You love sports and a priority on your budget that will give you much pleasure will be money spent on sports equipment. Consider using public recreation centres, pools, tennis courts and golf courses instead of using expensive and exclusive private facilities. You'll enjoy yourself just as much – and save money along the way.

You also love the outdoors. Try substituting hiking and picnicking at weekends for dining at restaurants or going to the cinema. Again, you'll enjoy yourself just as much, but at far lower cost.

You love to spend money on plants, and as like a few other artistically inclined members of the Zodiac you have green fingers, you will make your home attractive with hanging plants and shrubs. Take more cuttings from them and propagate your own plants rather than buying new ones – it's a satisfying way to save money.

When you buy clothing, you'll be happier with casual outdoor wear than with more formal attire. Save money in the long term by buying good quality clothes that will last rather than getting fashionable but less durable garments.

Many Sagittarians are artists, writers, craftspeople of one kind or another or teachers. They often have irregular incomes. Remember when you are preparing your budget to keep your estimates low, total what you expect for the year, not for a shorter term – too short term an estimate can give unbalanced figures and a distorted picture of your real earnings. And, impractical Sagittarians, remember that if your income should increase, don't be carried away – a pay rise always looks bigger than it is – until you take out taxes and other deductions. Compute only the net, take-home pay as your raise.

Last but not least, try to set aside a small but constant amount for savings. You are endeavouring to build up a reserve of several months' income, as a cushion to fall back on. Just because money isn't too important to you it doesn't mean you don't have to have any.

CAPRICORN (22nd December – 19th January)
You are the steely-eyed financial wizards of the Zodiac, practical and efficient, sometimes cautious, often bold – the merchant adventurers who create financial empires yet who rarely reveal the soft-hearted human waiting to be loved 'as a person'. Capricorns present the world with an image of austerity and stern purpose but underneath you are often softer than runny butter. For you, budgeting isn't a tedious task – it's more of a crusade, a holy duty. Your budget will be penny perfect, accurate and as detailed as your inventiveness can make it. Then you'll go through agonies trying to live up to it. Relax a little, no budget, however meticulously prepared, is perfect. There must be a degree of elasticity built into it. Ordinary mortals know this, but they aren't the omniscient perfectionists that you are and they expect to see the occasional error in their work. You don't.

How, for example, will you cope with inflation in your budget? Some items might rise just a few per cent – but you will spend a good fraction of your income on them. Others might rise dramatically, but you never buy them anyway – so it won't affect you. The lesson is that a budget must be flexible.

You have solid financial priorities. You will spend prodigally on a house because you know it is a good investment. A good car is less important to you, unless it's one of the few vehicles around that will appreciate in value. You would rather have an old banger than a new mid-priced car because you know just how expensive depreciation can be. You invariably take the long view in money matters.

You like to cook, you like to garden. You like to combine the two hobbies. Grow your own vegetables – it is a worthwhile investment of your time, will save you money and provide you with a pleasant hobby by the way. Grow your own decorative plants and flowers, perhaps even selling a few now and then.

Clothing isn't a major concern to you, so don't allocate it much importance when you are planning ahead. Children are important in your life so be prepared for major expenditures in schooling, hobbies, clothing and equipment.

Incidentally, a Capricorn friend is the only one we know who has been successful in teaching his pre-teen children how to handle credit cards successfully. The children are very confident with money, have had allowances since they could count, understand their obligations and buy their own clothing. It takes a Capricorn to monitor that kind of action – but he does, and the children are remarkably self-possessed about the whole thing. It is a classic case of a Capricorn, seeking to begin a dynasty, training his children in the use of what he sees as power-money.

Other priorities on your budget: gadgets and gimmicks. You love to spend on electronics, on stereo equipment and electric train sets for the children (but who plays with them most?). You regard magazines and books as important; you tend not to be too interested in travel, so you don't spend excessive amounts on holidays.

Budget to spend plenty on your car because even if you have an old one it will be kept mechanically excellent. Set aside a category in your savings scheme to cover unexpected emergencies – Capricorns love the sense of being in charge, of planning ahead and even a small but separate savings account for emergencies only will give you great pleasure. It goes without saying that it might even be useful ...

You enjoy eating, as you enjoy cooking. Make provision for eating out as part of your money management plans. You aren't usually adventurous in your eating habits, so it isn't a bad idea to patronise the same few restaurants frequently, so you will get better service, and more recognition and you

might also consider putting down a modest cellar of wine now
– for consumption several years hence. Your eating habits
will remain, and an investment now can mean some cheap but
fine wines to drink later.

AQUARIUS (20th January – 19th January)
Here's a non-mercenary sign which has everything – the
ability to be what you want, the ability to be loved by almost
everyone and the ability to make as much money as you need.
Aquarians, you've got it all.
   Except a budget.
   It's true of 99% of Aquarians that you are people lovers. You
have fine, creative and artistic temperaments, you neither
despise money nor love it – it's just something that happens to
be there. If you need some, along it will come. Generally you
have well-paid jobs, many more Aquarians than other Zodiac
denizens are self-employed (and needless to say are
successful), and the few who are short of cash are usually that
way from choice. But you could still use a properly thought
out budget. It can be a real liberating device for Aquarians.
You feel you don't want any rigid plan for your life, so you
tend to shy away from even common-sense ideas. You don't
want to feel trapped or cornered or pinned down by a page of
figures in black and white. Making a budget won't entrap you.
It will free your mind of everyday nuisances, like wondering
how much you really can afford to spend on books or
magazines today. You'll know what are your reasonable
allowances.
   Take a look at the things which Aquarians consider are
their real priorities: works of art, automobiles, electronics,
furniture, especially modern furniture of light woods or
plastics, learning, cinema, books, photography, precious
stones (sapphires are a favourite) sculpture, music, telephone
conversations, consciousness-raising experiences. Phew.
   Try and write those into a budget, you say. Yet if we

consider them again, apart from the odd item like cars and furniture, there are no real materialistic priorities. You Aquarians just aren't interested in acquiring goods or riches. You enjoy colour and movement, dance and music, talk and mysticism. You're too good for this place!

Make the optional part of your budget include reasonable funding for buying good quality art prints. You might consider opening an account at a good local art dealer's or art supplies shop and making a regular payment to them so you can buy that special work when you wish, instead of just wishing.

Allow enough for a special savings account for jewellery – again a long-term purchase – but one you will value all the more for the waiting. Set a certain monthly amount aside for furniture, and for your particular hobby. Many Aquarians enjoy sports like bird watching (Aquarians have an obsession with the air, with flying) or cycling, which lend themselves naturally to photography.

Include a generous amount for telephone calls, for stationery and postage and for newspaper and magazine subscriptions. Remember to allow for buying books – art books especially can be expensive and several of those in a month can make a dent in an ill-prepared budget. Music is another priority for the well-balanced Aquarian budget – so allow for concert tickets, records, and instruments or instrument rental costs.

It might sound a little formidable, but you Aquarians will live modestly in many ways to indulge your spiritual tastes. You enjoy but can live without expensive meals, huge houses and large cars. Some Aquarians are quite religious and spend much time and energy working for their church or chapel. If this means you, remember to allow for church and charitable contributions in your monthly budget.

Remember, too, that creating a budget is one of the few creative things an Aquarian can do that is not interpretive. You must stick to the facts – not your ideas of what they should be. Once done, the bones of your new found financial independence will be set. Just flesh them with your actions. Good luck.

PISCES (20th February – 20th March)
Pisceans, here we are about to do you a wonderful service – we will introduce you to a glamorous, wonderful thing called a *budget*! You can tell all your friends how you found it – it just followed you home and was so adorable you felt it would be unkind to let it loose. And after a while, you came to love it, it needed you and by golly, it did you some service, too!

Generally you are unhappy to be handling lumps of cash, you dislike the responsibility and you feel that somehow it isn't your job, you aren't capable of it, there's a 'R' in the month – any excuse. Well, the fact is that once you start finding out about your money-handling talents, you'll never want to stop.

Once established, a good money management plan will liberate you from the feast-and-famine financial life you have been suffering. You might no longer enjoy the peaks of emotion you have come to associate with a spending spree, but neither will you suffer the miseries of paying it all off later. If you establish the savings plan we suggest – putting away a modest 5% of your net each month – you will be able, quicker than you would guess, to go out on a spending spree but without the morning-after blues.

Let's take another look at what you should put high on your list of spending priorities.

You enjoy quality goods, and rightly so. You are careful with your possessions because you have a streak of materialism in you and know the value of things you purchase. A good car will last you a long time. A cheaper car will also last longer than it would in other hands, but the quality equipment is well worth the difference as it will not depreciate as fast over its longer life. Cameras and optical goods – binoculars and microscopes – are popular Piscean buys. You enjoy examining things, and will use the equipment often – so buy quality goods. Spend money on your home too. You tend to stay in an area for years, so you might as well enjoy the facilities instead of scrimping in this part of the budget. It isn't a bad investment, either.

Try to reduce your medical expenditures. You don't always need to be a private patient, because frankly you are often a little too sensitive about your own possible ailments. Be harder on yourself and also do take a little more exercise – Pisceans are notorious for their reluctance to keep themselves in shape.

Make allowances for spending on education. Many Pisceans prefer to send their children to private schools, and an insurance policy taken out soon enough can mean a useful lump sum at a time you need it. Consider taking out a policy when your child is born, to pay university costs later.

Reduce your expenditure on drinks. Many Pisceans drink like, well, like a fish. It isn't good for you, it's expensive and it's something you can save money on. If you must drink, consider cheaper brands of liquor for mixed drinks – you can't tell the difference most of the time anyway. Drink wine or beer instead of spirits – you'll feel the differences both in your health and in your bank balance.

Chapter Three
Credit and easing the repayment pains

'Ah, take the cash and let the credit go,
Nor heed the rumble of a distant drum!'

Edward Fitzgerald

Credit is both boon and bane. It can put material goods within our reach just when we need them, but an unwise use of its temptations can cause us considerable financial trouble.

Let's look at some of the ground rules for establishing credit – who gets it, how you can improve your rating, what the bank, loan company or creditor generally looks for.

First of all, there are the credit bureaux. They collect information about borrowers and sell it to retailers, banks, credit card companies – anybody who lends money. When you apply for a loan, for a car lease or for a job it's almost certain that a credit report will be obtained on you. Contrary to popular belief, you are not rated as a good or bad credit risk on any kind of points scale. The bureaux collect from all kinds of sources, including merchants with whom you have had or presently have credit, and from other records, information about your spending and loan habits. They consider your address, occupation, employer and earnings. They weigh your records of employment, marriage, patterns of living – whether you move often, for example – and repayment patterns on previous loans. Generally, if you have had credit before and have paid off the loan on time you will be in good shape for another loan. Some lenders – large stores, for example – are happy if you repay charges within a month or so. Others – banks, especially – tend to demand repayment on the due date.

Generally, you are assessed as credit worthy on several counts:

* your personal traits – of honesty, trustworthiness, responsibility and soundness of judgement. These are revealed through factual records and patterns of repayment of previous loans as well as a look at your personal job and credit history.

* your financial muscle. Can you repay the loan? Do you have enough room in your budget? What sort of job, with what prospects, have you?

* your realizable assets. A home filled with expensive furniture, your bank balance, cars, jewellery, any tangible and valuable property that could be regarded as collateral, these are factors every creditor likes to know about.

Good points in your favour are usually these:

* stability of employment – have you been with the same employer for a reasonable length of time, or are you a working butterfly, flitting from job to job?

* charge accounts – do you (a) have any? (b) pay them off on time? Two yesses will mean bonus points for you in a credit rating examination.

* home and family – do you own your home? Do you have a family? Again, more bonus points for yesses. But don't despair if you rent – if you have lived at your address for some time that too is an indication of stability.

* banking: if you are applying to a bank for a mortgage or loan, do you have an account with them? If you have, it's a major plus.

What counts against you when seeking a good credit reference?

* lack of identity – if you can't properly identify yourself, with a birth certificate, driving licence, insurance number or other documents.

* unstable job – if you travel from town to town, do

seasonal work, are in a volatile industry or have a poor history of staying with one job.

* unstable address – if you are a transient, live in an hotel or boarding house, have only recently moved into your present address. However, if you can show you have a long history of living in one place, fairly recently, you can offset this disadvantage.

* applying for a loan away from home – someone from Glasgow who applies for a loan with a Manchester bank is asking for queries – unless they are presently living in Manchester. Loan officers look with suspicion on applicants from elsewhere.

* not having a guarantor if you are a minor applying for a loan. Young people, with smaller earnings and less settled lives are not favoured loan customers. They actually tend to be good credit risks, but there is a historical bias against them – so be prepared to have an adult co-signer.

What should you do if you lose your credit cards? Millions of pounds are stolen each year through credit card fraud. Consider this list of do's and don't's.

* do list all your cards, with numbers, expiration dates, etc. List addresses of the issuers, telephone numbers for emergency bureaux. Keep this list in a safe place – but not in your purse or wallet.

* do sign all your cards. Destroy any that are out of date by cutting them in half.

* don't lend your card to anyone – it's an offence.

* do check to see you still have them all at least once a week.

* do ensure you get your card back each time you use it – more people lose cards that way than any other!

* don't leave your card, driving licence, etc. in the glove box of your car – credit cards and identification are as tempting as cash to a thief.

If you follow these principles, you will reduce the potential damage of losing a card. Most credit companies put a limit on your liability, but if you lose several cards at once that limit can be fairly high. Just remember – your card is plastic cash. Treat it like pound notes.

Before we launch into the individual signs and how each treats credit and the whole process of repaying debts, there is one word of advice on repayments that applies to every Zodiac sign.

Some companies specialise in offering to relieve your debt burdens by paying off all your small debts – and you repay them with one monthly lump payment. This 'debt lumping' can be a dreadful mistake for you. It will not save you money. The fact is that these companies often charge up to 33% interest. Do not be fooled by some hard-selling salesman who claims all your worries will end. You are simply paying out even more – and the company might disappear into the night with your payments anyway.

Do not confuse these companies with legitimate bank or debt consolidation loans available from principled companies – but do be wary. Too often these easy ways out are only unscrupulous schemes to part you from your money.

Once you have earned your credit and used it to buy the goods you needed, you face the next step – making repayments. If you know you own strengths, implicit in you since birth thanks to your Zodiac sign, you will be able to make the repayments less painful. Let's look, sign by sign, at how each member of the Zodiac is best suited to pay off debts – and why.

AIRES (21st March – 19th April)
Enterprising, adventurous Ariens, you love to use credit because it satisfies your innate sense of immediacy. You see something, you want it, you obtain it thanks to a bank loan officer's smile – and your signature. Then comes the reckoning. You have two or three years to pay off the loan.

Your spirit quails. You wonder if the new appliance will even last that long. You want to return it.

Do this: think of the repayments as being a brand new enterprise, an exercise in your skill, perseverance and determination. You have the quality of tenacity to pay off a loan, little by little, once you decide you should. You would prefer to make one grand gesture and pay it off at once, from your carefully-built savings, but then there would be no purpose in taking out the loan anyway.

Treat the repayment as an exercise in tenacity, skill and as a challenge to yourself. Draw a chart to show your progress. Yours won't be a charted failure – it will be a triumphant chart of success. And you'll learn something about budgeting along the way – because you will have to plan this financial outlay along with all the others.

TAURUS (20th April – 21st May)

Taureans have an affinity for the steady life, the steady job, the steady repayment schedule. The chances are that when you went to see the loan officer you knew as much as he did about interest rates, repayment terms and how best to finance your deal. For you, the neatest and most satisfactory way is to have repayments made by banker's standing order. Every month you will have that same amount painlessly taken out of your current account, transferred across to the loan account and all that you will see will be black figures on a crisp white sheet. No cash, no mess, no fuss.

A pleasant way for you to boost your morale as the repayments are made for you is to view them as a banker views them. These are figures which must eventually balance, but which in the meantime can give you pleasure as you watch the total mount up, and the debt decrease. Find a fellow Taurean to mention it to, oh so casually, of course. You'll both glow with pleasure as you bemoan the problems you have meeting all those awful payments and you'll gloomily console each other with White's Law (that things are never as bad as they turn out to be).

Anyway, fortunate Taureans, you are among those rare and wonderful creatures who can enjoy dealing with money, debts and borrowings.

GEMINI (22nd May – 20th June)

Geminis consider money unimportant. You're either prodigal or the world's most intelligent people – who knows which? Your ideal way of dealing with debts is simply to raid the savings and pay it off at once. You might consider an option or two, Gemini. Try either using some of those savings in the first place to negotiate a cash price for the goods (some credit card debts are impulse buys that you might not have bought if you'd had to go and get cash from the bank). Using cash has another advantage – you can usually buy something cheaper for cash than any other way.

However, you will often want something *now*, not next week. The credit card or the charge account is a useful way of gaining a month's credit, free of charge. At certain times you can actually make savings that way – a card will let you use your good credit to buy at sales time and pay a month later.

Another option for you is to have the bank deduct a monthly amount to pay off the loan, or to have it withdrawn directly from your pay cheque, before you get your hands on it.

Try to understand your own duality of attitude to money and try to make allowance for it. You can play one of your diverse characters off against the other – but who will win on any given day is another matter. Gemini, you're a puzzle but a loveable one.

CANCER (21st June – 22nd July)

Bankers love to see you walk into their temples of money,

Cancerians. You are the solid, dependable, reliable, slightly mother-hennish clients they want. If you are late with a loan repayment you'll worry. You would rather go short of food than feel you had let someone down. Your credit purchases are likely to be solid and worthwhile, just like yourself. You spend on household goods, on cars, on things with a value. You don't usually splash out on luxury holidays or wonderful clothing for yourself (although you will be tempted to do it for a member of your family). It means that the loan officer knows he has security for his loan to you. After all, he can always come around and repossess the car or the furniture – it's a tough task to scrape a suntan from the face of a spent-up holidaymaker.

So, you have no trouble getting loans because they are for worthwhile investments. Do you have difficulties repaying them? Perhaps you do on occasion, but the general pattern of your financial life is stable. You are well able to plan ahead – you fret and fuss over purchases for weeks before you make them.

Your repayment pattern shows that you have the self-discipline to make small, steady, repayments on time. You are Moon Children and you could purchase the moon, given an instalment plan, because you have the Crab's tenacity of purpose and will keep paying off your lunar estates until they are all yours.

LEO (23rd July – 22nd August)
Your friends might admire your new clothes and jewellery but they probably shudder just a little inside, knowing you'll be descending on them for a free meal or some small loan while you pay for them.

Leos have the royal gift of being above such matters as mere money. You want a new suit – buy it, worry about it all later. The 'buy now pay later' slogans of the Fifties were coined just for you. You use credit mercilessly and live larger than life right now – tomorrow can go hang, there will be some way you can use your splendid wits to escape the creditors' noose. And that's the way it all too often happens.

But just once couldn't you try to live within your means? You could then use your wonderful brains to think of useful things, instead of merely working to escape the county court, or using all your fatal charm to extract some favour or loan from a long-suffering friend.

Consider that if you simply drew in your horns for a month, lived modestly, then resumed your normal lifestyle, you would then be a month in credit instead of a month in debt. Instead of considering what you can sell that you don't need, to pay off some delicious dinner long since digested and forgotten by all except the restaurant who wants paying, think of the joys of being solvent. . . .

Pretend that paying off bills is a regal way of distributing largesse, of making a grand gesture. You are really above all that nasty business of debts, so why not make an effort to use the lessons of budgeting and get on to an even financial keel? Once there, you will have more opportunity to be open handed and open hearted as usual – but this time you will be doing it with your own money.

Make a crash course of paying back your debts, at considerable cost to yourself, but at temporary cost only – and then start again with a clean sheet and a budget plan.

VIRGO (23rd August – 22nd September)
You are the responsible, sensible planners of the Zodiac, analytical and studious, creative and careful. You know that credit is a potential problem if it isn't used properly. So you are able to coolly calculate just what you need from credit, how you can best use it and what it will cost you for the convenience. Often you'll reject the idea – and will save cash until you can buy outright what you want. Sometimes you will, of course, use a loan to buy the needed goods.

You are responsible and thrifty, you can repay loans easily by using your patience and making on-time repayments over a moderately long period. Sometimes, though, you rebel and go on a modest spending binge. You'll come home and confess to your spouse that you have just bought an expensive coffee grinder, which although not totally useless is more than a modest luxury. Then, for weeks you do mental penance.

Don't feel bad, Virgo perfectionist. *We* know you're human, even if you don't. It's not a sin to have hire purchase debts, although you don't like them. You have an innate talent for quietly and efficiently making repayments, without drama or fuss.

LIBRA (23rd September – 22nd October)
You Librans are like your Virgo sisters in many way. You are meticulous, self-contained, independent and efficient. Most of you hate the very thought of taking out a loan to buy something – you'd rather do without. Your idea of coping with major household purchases isn't to visit your friendly loan officer. It's to squirrel away change from housekeeping, or the loose change in your pockets at the end of the day, putting it all into a box, until you have enough to deposit at the bank. Then you'll start all over again, making another deposit several months later – until one day you have the whole amount you need for that purchase.

Some Librans prefer the Secondhand Rose Routine. They hardly ever purchase new things but always seek out the meticulously-kept, previously-owned goods they want and buy them for a fraction of their purchase price when new. They find them advertised by Taurus and Cancer people who are refurbishing their homes.

You tend to repay loans early, to maintain scrupulous records of debts and even to have old receipts, time-lapsed guarantees and a bundle of school reports from every year since you were five all stowed neatly away in a bureau. You don't need organising – the credit bureaux need your help instead. Paying back loans isn't a pain for you – it's a joy to get those untidy, someone-has-a-claim-on-me feelings paid off.

SCORPIO (23rd October – 21st November)
Here's a sign that won't take half-measures. Scorpio, you use credit and loans to achieve your ends. You enjoy using money and credit cards, charge accounts and bank balances are meat and drink to you.

You don't see your best course of paying back those debts as pulling in your horns. Not likely. You will go out aggressively and earn extra money by taking another job, by moonlighting. It appeals to you because you are restless and inventive. You want to get ahead and you don't see how cramping your style by spending less is going to help. So you don't spend less – you simply earn more.

Usually you don't tell your colleagues about your other financial activities. They might, they frequently do, wonder about why you are tired sometimes during the day, and how the devil did you manage to purchase that new car when they simply can't make ends meet, but you never tell. You like the secrecy, the sense of power you get from keeping a secret from them. Be careful you don't let your sense of privacy turn into contempt for them because they don't do the same. You can have a biting wit – and it will alienate good friends.

The secret then for Scorpios is just that – have a secret hoard of money, or have a private source of income. You will benefit both financially and mentally.

SAGITTARIUS (22nd November – 21st December)
Wicked astrologers say that Sagittarians like you have strong shoulder muscles from shrugging philosophically when things go wrong. Well, you know, as did Mahatma Gandhi,

that there is more to life than increasing its speed, and you are idealistic enough to believe that things will improve.

Often you need these suits of mental armour, because you attract more than your fair share of problems yet you stay optimistic. Sagittarians are tough.

You are always liable to incur debts from your love of recreation. Younger Sagittarians are sports fanatics, older ones are active, mentally if not always physically. You'll spend on a trip to watch a sporting event, to see a rare bird or to watch for seals off the coast. Curiously, much of your spending is linked not to material goods, but to the cost of indulging your semi-spiritual appetites.

The day always comes when you have to pay the piper. If you haven't got the money, and that isn't too rare an event, you don't get upset. You shrug philosophically and reason 'Well, I had the benefits, it's only fair that I pay for them now.' And you do. It might mean that you cash in an insurance policy, or take a part-time job for a month or two, or even cut back on household expenses to liberate some extra cash.

This sense of responsibility makes you a splendid loan customer. But why not make matters a little easier for yourself? Instead of spending before and making repayments later, why not try to scratch together a financial cushion first? It's not too radical an idea, Sagittarians. Think of it as earning the right to spend the money instead of paying for the privilege of having spent it.

CAPRICORN (22nd December – 19th January)
Capricorn, the customs officer of the Zodiac, stern and upright, unbending and moral, when would you *ever* incur debts? You are calculatingly business-like and you'd incur debts whenever it suited your purpose best. You usually get the best deals that are available, you're economical so don't waste money on frivolities although you will spend freely on a spouse.

However, let's assume you have debts. How best to repay them? Two easy ways spring to mind for Capricorns. Either you should have a fixed amount withheld from your pay each month, to be paid directly into a bank account or to the loan company, or – and this is a popular suggestion for most Capricorns – you should look at your possessions and decide what you could sell to finance the purchase of your newest need.

You see, you Capricorns regard money as purely a business tool. It is the same view you hold of your possessions (except for your hobby equipment). They are investments, assets and nothing more. They have little or no emotional appeal for you. You rarely say 'I couldn't sell that – it was my mother's.' You are more likely to say 'I'll sell that, it was my mother's, therefore it is practically a valuable antique.'

Possessions are to be used, you believe. You have the same attitude to them that an otter has to a pool of water. It must be churned up, used and made alive. It is no use as a still, peaceful, mirror-like sheet. Water is for disporting in. You Capricorns regard money as something similar – a medium to be used, not left to stagnate.

So, to ease the repayment pangs – remember to either set up a special fund, painlessly withheld in a businesslike way, or consider selling off one or two assets.

AQUARIUS (20th January – 19th February)
You Aquarians rarely have any pay-back pains when it becomes time to settle your debts. You just don't mind handing over your hard-earned money. You're realistic enough to know that the promised land always looks better from a distance but diplomatic enough not to mention it to the poor pilgrims struggling to reach it.

And money for them *is* the promised land. For you, it's a useful tool not vital enough to lose sleep over. (Although when it gets to the point where we examine who has and who hasn't, we find that Aquarians generally have it, and plenty, even if you didn't try to gather it.)

However, let's assume you are temporarily embarrassed by a lack of funds – not to put too fine a point on it, you're overdrawn at the bank, you have a sheaf of bills that would choke an alligator and the red ring on the calendar has long since passed the first day of the month. Most signs of the Zodiac would press the panic button. Not you.

You cool and progressive Aquarians will simply find a spare-time job. You'll earn extra money. You'll also inform your creditors simply and politely that there might be a short delay, but normal service will be resumed – and you'll quickly, quietly and efficiently set about bringing home some bacon.

You'll often cut back drastically on home operating expenses unless that causes too much discomfort to yourself, but you'll find a way to make money – and quickly. You are the best equipped of the entire Zodiac to think your way out of a financial quagmire before it swallows you, and that's just what you will do. Just remember that your natural option is simply to earn a little more money.

PISCES (20th February – 20th March)
Of all the signs of the Zodiac, the cards are most stacked against you, Pisceans, when it comes to handling debts. You see, you have a natural talent for procrastination and you're always likely to ignore a debt in the hope that it will evaporate. It's absolutely the worst thing you can do. Delaying tactics and money hardly mix and your credit rating will suffer. So you have to attack your repayment problems at the root – which is the time you spend getting around to repaying them.

Generally, Pisces people don't have very bad money problems. You might feel that yours are awful, but you do have a slight tendency to pessimism and caution. By and large, Pisces people are cautious about taking on responsibility and they will tread with great precision. So, you don't often recklessly blitz your way into a minefield of debts.

Once you are in, don't delay. Even if you can't repay at once, at least let your creditors know why – you'll be surprised how accommodating they can be. Your best repayment plan generally is to have a standing order at the bank, to have them take out a certain amount each month for loan repayments. That way you will avoid late payment charges and damaged credit.

So that's the secret for you Pisceans: plan ahead, expect credit card or charge account debts – and set up a section of your budget to cope with them.

Chapter Four
What to do and where to live

'Oh let us love our occupations,
bless the squire and his relations,
live upon our daily rations,
and always know our proper stations.'

Charles Dickens.

Our proper stations aren't what they used to be. Since the Industrial Revolution we no longer adopt the traditional occupations of our forebears, we are a mobile and a socially changeable society. Certainly, what we do is as much of a social marker as ever it was, but today we all have the opportunity to change. This chapter is intended to spell out which choices can be best for which Zodiac signs and where you should live for the happiest and most satisfying life.

French researchers have established that certain Zodiac signs are better suited to certain occupations than others and they found statistically significant loading of certain signs in certain occupations, which seemed to indicate that an unconscious human selection was being made by those signs. Cancerians, for example, make excellent caterers, Leos make actors and Virgos make engineers. Of course, not all Leos are actors, but a trend is discernible in that actors are Leos than any other sign. Astrologers have long known by empirical means that certain signs have certain gifts and are most successful in areas which allow them to use those gifts.

Those gifts are not everything, however. Certain places are more favourable for certain signs as residences, certain lifestyles suit particular signs better. It's not unreasonable to assume that a Leo, with his love of the bright lights and razzle dazzle, with a penchant for clothes and being seen, will be less than happy to be plonked down in a backwater Somerset village. (Although, being a Leo, he'll quickly establish himself as the village's honorary squire and bore any captive audience stiff with far-fetched tales of his triumphs on the boards, in the boardrooms or the bedrooms of the distant city.)

Of course, relatively few people who read this chapter and who discover that their ideal home lies in the foothills of the Pyrenees are likely to up stakes and move there instantly. Equally, an antique dealer who is advised that his true profession is as a sailor is unlikely to change. There is, however, some practical advice hidden in the chapter. You might consider taking a holiday at your astrologically-ideal spot – who knows, one day you might retire there. Or you might discover that your preferred profession will fit with your hobby or give you an idea for a new one.

At least, here is some food for imaginative musings – what might have been and what possibly still could be. And it isn't outside the realms of possibility that once you have the knowledge you might see an opportunity arise which could lead to future potential hitherto undreamed of.

Let's look and consider who is best suited for what – and where best to live.

ARIES (21st March – 19th April)
Your adventurous instincts, self assertiveness, initiative and leadership make certain professions ideal for you. You love exploring, be it across the world, or as geologists or psychiatrists, examining the outer edges of our knowledge.

Rams make good butchers and surgeons – especially of anything to do with the head. You are fine brain surgeons, ear, nose and throat specialists, barbers or hairdressers, eye doctors or opticians. You make firemen – or any occupation connected with fire – safety officers, blacksmiths, steel workers. You are often dentists, hat makers or hat sellers, hardware dealers or gangsters. You do well in advertising and marketing, in public relations and counselling. You enjoy being behind the scenes at entertainment events, at athletic meets, sports and promotions – from book fairs to the Olympics. You'll find good opportunities in any kind of selling company related to construction – from architecture to surveying companies; also cement manufacturing, chemical companies, the armed forces, the police, security guard companies, uniformed jobs of most kinds – porters, ticket collectors, commissionaires and railway guards. Other professions and occupations: detective, canvasser, fire fighter, pop musician, handyman, carpenter, gold assayer, distiller, water engineer, lobster fisherman, poacher, lumber-jack, store owner, gunsmith and beauty consultant. Any of these are good ways for you to earn money – and enjoy doing it.

Where to live: England is our first choice for you roaming Aries – a patchwork of green and gold, a maze of city streets and country lanes, varied and crowded, empty and unchanging. It's a lot of territory packed into a small space, offering both variety – something close to your Arien soul – and convenience.

However, there are other alternatives. France and Germany are ideal, for similar reasons as England – they combine the rural and the industral so both your peace-loving soul and commercial initiative will find peace. Other choices include Poland, Denmark, Syria, Israel and Egypt.

Cities that will suit you include any of the northern England industrial towns (especially those which fostered the woollen trade), Leicester and the west Midlands, Utrecht, Padua, Verona, Florence, Cracow, Capua, Hamburg and Munich.

You Rams are happiest around the stimulation of commerce, the cut and thrust of the market place. Try to settle where you can at least occasionally enjoy that mental exercise. One last word – don't be too impatient about finding your ideal home.

TAURUS (20th April – 21st May)
Those born under the sign of the Bull have sterling qualities for the working world. You make excellent executives – thanks to your painstaking approach – you're super civil servants, conscientious and caring public officials and natural bankers. But these are not the only areas in which you'll excel. You will make money and enjoy it as artists, beauticians, concert organisers, courtesans, club leaders, dancers and decorators. You will be successful as dress-makers, entertainers, festival managers, florists, haber-dashers, hairdressers, hotel keepers, jewellers, musicians and orchestra leaders. You also make superb opera singers, poets, tailors, theatre owners, upholsterers and wardrobe mistres-ses. In fact, you make excellent mistresses of the other kind – because you have a strong streak of sensuality in your character. Taurus is ruled by Venus. Necklace manufacturers, tie designers, hangmen, clerical collar manufacturers, even stranglers are often found in the ranks of you Taureans – because you have a natural affinity for the throat. You make fine coin dealers, confectioners, cooks, conscientious farmers or farm hands, landscape designers, golf course or garden maintenance people. You love flowers and precious stones and stables – anything connected to their manufacture, upkeep, design or handling will serve you well.

Above everything towers the colossus of your talent – as a handler of money. You are financiers, bankers, loan officers, treasurers and cashiers. It is your Taurean gift – so try to work with it.

Where you should live: Taureans' best countries are the Soviet Union, Poland, Sweden and Switzerland. Ireland, too, has lots of attractions for you, but the banking community in Switzerland makes that country nearly irresistible for you –

even if it's only for holidays. It has the virtues you yourself possess – it's organised, neat, well-run and efficient. Less orthodox Taureans might consider Iran – the Ayatollah Khomeini was born under the same astrological influences as you – and some few of you could happily settle in South Africa.

Florida, Dublin, Eastbourne, Hastings, Lucerne, Leipzig and Moscow are all good places for you to live or visit. Taureans with relatives in Australia will enjoy going there, and the sun-seeking Taureans among you will enjoy Cyprus, Greece, Maryland, and Parma.

Wherever you travel, you will be organised. You love to read about your destination before you leave, you conscientiously pack the various medicines and an array of appropriate clothing. And wherever you go, your solid worth, your patent honesty and dependability will endear you to people you meet.

GEMINI (22nd May – 20th June)

Alexander Pope drew the character of Gemini when he wrote:

'With too much quickness ever to be taught,

with too much thinking to have common thought.'

He decided your true occupations without even considering you – you need variety, spice and fast-moving, thinking-on-your-feet occupations. Any occupations which bring you into contact with people are ideally suited to your talents. You make excellent reception and sales people, public relations or press officers, tour guides and lecturers. You enjoy displaying your wits, and any of the communication disciplines, writing, politics, television presenting, university lecturing, school teaching, are wonderful outlets for your abilities. You also make excellent scientists and investigators.

Run a finger down this list and see some of your special areas: advertising executive, architect, astronomer, book keeper, clerk, debater, diplomat, conman, dictator, educator, forger, grocer, journalist, governess, dancer, dental hygienist, juggler, lecturer, messenger, museum guide, mimic, notepaper designer, peddler, postal clerk, printer, publisher, rabbi, secretary, storekeeper, stool pigeon, spy, student, tennis player, translator, seamstress, social butterfly, wit, medium, geographer, crusader, computer operator, stockbroker, telephone operator and railway worker.

Deciding where you want to live is not easy for you, Gemini. You want two worlds – and a fast commute between them. On any given day you will want to live quietly in the country – for an hour or two, until your restless spirit decides the bustle of the city is your real metier. Belgium, the cockpit of Europe, isn't a bad choice for you. But you can also try other locations: the West Country, the United States, with its wide, wonderful and varied differences; Egypt, Wales, Africa, Armenia, Eastern Canada with its Gemini-like divisions.

Other likely places include Central America, with the vast social differences there; New York – a collection of villages in a city; Nuremburg, Rio de Janeiro, Saudi Arabia, Versailles, where old and new cultures exisit peacefully side by side; Plymouth and Melbourne.

Wherever you stay, however, you probably won't ever feel settled. Yours is a wandering star, so plan to travel, at least for your holidays, to alleviate that itch.

CANCER (21st June – 22nd July)

The best jobs for you, industrious Crabs, involve frugality, industry and conscientiousness. You enjoy work connected with homemaking, so there's a whole area for you to consider. Specific occupations that suit you well: baker, brewer, caterer, dairy farmer, fisherman, housewife, janitor, laundryman, lighthouse keeper (because you like to bring people home safely) air traffic controller or bus driver (for the same reasons), obstetrician, restauranteur (a favourite Cancerian fantasy), sailor, dry cleaning operative, silversmith, waiter, washerwoman, watchman. Anything to do with hotels or motels suits you: hotel keeper, desk clerk, waitress. People who look after buildings – janitor, landlord, builder, maintenance man, housepainter. Also, kitchen ware designer, milkman, oceanographer, deep-sea diver, plumber, property developer, caravan manufacturer or salesperson. (Cancerians like caravans – they are their shells, portable yet domestic). And there are other occupations, like shrimp fisherman, weather forecaster and washing machine salesperson – all connected with water, your ruling element.

Where to live and work: most Cancerians are very patriotic and put down domestic roots that are deep and long-lasting. They might travel, but their hearts and memories remain with their original homes and the places where they were brought up. Scotland, Holland, Burgundy, Africa, Germany, Paraguay, China, USA and Canada are favourite areas.

Places in which you will be happy include Amsterdam – a city founded on and around water, like Venice, another favourite; Istanbul, Milan, York, St. Andrews, Manchester and most parts of Lancashire; California, central Canada, Cadiz, Chicago, Genoa, Idaho, Iraq, New Hampshire, New Zealand, New Mexico, Pittsburg, Stockholm, Tunis, Virginia and Llanberis, Wales.

LEO (23rd July – 22nd August)
Extrovert emperors of the Zodiac, you are always slightly larger than life and loved for it. You love people – they love you. You have so many good traits that it would almost embarrass you to have to read them. Of course you know that your true occupation is acting. That isn't new – after all, much of your working day is spent acting, anyway – whether you are a barrister at the Old Bailey or a diver working underwater on a North Sea oil rig. You enjoy an audience but you really don't need one, because you are your own most critical audience,

and you act accordingly. Let's look at some of your best avenues of occupation: drama, sports, high office. You make actors and animators, ballroom dancers and bosses. You often are attracted to dancing – be it rock and roll or ballet – because you can capture the limelight. You can bluff and con people, you make excellent biologists, charity organisers, front office people. You're natural celebrities, dictators, foremen, game players, gamblers – but not usually prosperous ones, just entertaining ones – psychic healers, doctors, prime ministers, cabinet ministers, union leaders, any kind of leader, teacher, university don, wizard (a wonderful profession for a Leo – drama, dash, flair and the odd dragon) or warlock. Then there are the amusement, entertainment, cabaret type jobs – from running donkey rides on the beach to managing giant amusement parks. Leos, you make wonderful bookmakers, stockbrokers, boardroom wizards, filmstars, foresters, commandoes – the dashing, cravatted type rather than the anonymous hero – lovers, managers, gigolos. You do anything with flair, and more things with flair than people would believe possible.

Where to live: ideally for you Leos, a castle, schloss or palazzo. You will live happily in a ruined baronial home, with rising damp and falling plaster. Something grand, or at least once-grand, is better suited to your tastes than something sensible, cramped and cosy.

Consider these options: France, Italy, Bohemia, Rumania, Sicily, Venetia, the Alps in general. Think of a suitable pied á terre in Hollywood or Rome, Prague or Syracuse; Damascus would suit you well, as would Bath or Bristol, Portsmouth or Chicago; Alaska, Berlin, Blackpool, Bolton – a much underrated town close to our hearts. Then there are places like Western Canada – you'll love Vancouver – Chaldea, Hawaii (but avoid Oahu – try the out islands), Jerusalem and Madagascar, Miami and Las Vegas, San Francisco – another city close to our hearts, but avoid the Tenderloin – and San Diego.

VIRGO (23rd August – 22nd September)
This is the sign that invariably gives astrologers trouble.
When we designed a line of perfumes for the Zodiac, the one
the perfumier couldn't decide upon was the Virgo. You see,
you're a subtle sign, you aren't bold and brash, brassy and
bigoted. You are a sign of service, of self-effacement. You are,
in a word, the butlers of the Zodiac. You're discreet and
perfectionist, quiet and efficient. You enjoy doing something
quietly and well and that's what you do. Accounts and
accountants, administrators and people who deal with
animals, beekeepers and book keepers; butlers and butter
makers; cheese manufacturers and chess players; chemists
and civil servants – these are all splendid outlets for the Virgo
talents. Clothing trade work attracts you – fitting and
tailoring, selling and designing. It's all aimed at the pleasure
of others, and quiet satisfaction in a subtle job well done.
Craftsmen and literary critics; dairy farmers, dental hygien-
ists and dieticians, these are Virgo occupations, too.
Also, doctors, draughtsmen, editors, filing clerks, food
industry workers, gardeners, chefs, grocers, haberdashers,
public health officers, book or manuscript illustrators,
librarians, maidservants, cartographers or mapsellers,
microbiologists, naval personnel, nurserymen or nursery
nurses, osteopaths, pharmacists, physical education teachers,
physicians, poultrymen, restauranteurs (a secret dream you
share with Cancerians) or scientists. Anything to do with
needlework, sewing, dressmaking, tailoring, clothes designing or fashion is in your nature, and you also make wonderful
veterinary surgeons, animal trainers, and zoological gardens
workers.

Where to live: you enjoy places with interest all their own,
places where you can quietly go about your business. You like
the industrial north of England, the great cities where life can
resemble existence in an anthill simply because you enjoy
the anonymity, the sense of worth you get from working and
knowing that all those around you are busy, active and

working too. Not for you the hedonism of the South of France. You are no social butterfly – you have an innate sense of self-worth that only allows you to enjoy a holiday for a week or so at a time before you start wishing you were back home, being busy again.

Try the Aleutian Islands, Alaska, Assyria, Babylonia, Basel, Brindisi, California, Cheltenham, Corinth, Croatia, Egypt, Heidelburg, Jerusalem, Lyons, Maidstone, Maidenhead, the Amazon Basin, Mozambique, Moscow, the Fens, especially Norwich, Ely or anywhere slightly out of the way. Then there are places like Padua, Paris, Perpignan, Philadelphia, Romney Marshes, Strasbourg, all of Switzerland, Toulouse, the Virgin Islands and Zimbabwe.

Really, where you Virgoans live isn't as vital as it can be for some other signs. You calmly avoid stress, you cope with hot spots coolly and in a detached way and you are so self possessed even you wish sometimes you could let your hair down more easily. It means you can live almost anywhere and enjoy yourself – because there are plenty of other people around and you enjoy helping them.

LIBRA (23rd September – 22nd October)
You are the nurses of the Zodiac, soft of hand, gentle of voice and manner. You make diplomats, politicians, analysts and wonderful wives or husbands. You are considerate, caring and careful. Yet under that caring exterior, there lurks a lustful, loving person. There is another side to Librans – the loving, giving, wanton side they rarely display. Let's consider some of the occupations for which you are best suited and see if you don't agree: yours is a world of actors and actresses, of adrenal glands, affection and admiration. You work well with antiques and objets d'art, you adore bedrooms and boudoirs, boutiques and china, crystal and confectionery, cooperage and breweries. You make fine cosmeticians, coppersmiths, decorators and painters. You are excellent

diamond merchants, diplomats, fashionable fops and florists. You would be fine furriers, grand generals, great golfers and happy hookers (be it on the field or off). Other congenial occupations: harbourmaster, musician, interior decorator, jeweller, judge, magistrate, milliner, company director, portrait painter, politician, receptionist, secretary, theatrical dresser, salesman, sailor, tree trimmer, gynaecologist, wigmaker, women's wear manufacturer or salesperson or woodsman.

Where to live in true Libran fashion: Antwerp in Belgium, Argentina, Austria, anywhere close to the Black Sea, Charleston, West Virginia, Chicago, China – but only for a visit, Copenhagen, Freiburg in the Black Forest, Frankfurt-am-Main, Japan, Johannesburg, Lisbon, Fresno, California, Nottingham and Pittsburgh. Best choice: Dunedin, New Zealand.

SCORPIO (23rd October – 21st November)

Whatever people can say about you, Scorpions, you aren't colourless or boring. You might be a trifle secretive, you're usually highly-sexed, you often have a fierce temper and you're generally a little too possessive. You are a positive person. You either succeed dramatically or fail miserably. You know, as few others do, that the middle of the road is a good place to get run over. You seek out professions that have a degree of flair, of centre stage, of danger and opportunity too. Medicine, the military and anything that hints of secrecy all attract you. Yours was the sign that produced the medieval alchemists, and today produces the electronic wizards who examine sub-atomic structures, who develop new drugs, who create mind-dazzling weaponry.

You make wonderful chemists, coroners, cemetery and crematorium workers, doctors and surgeons, medical researchers and pathologists, nurses, nightwatchmen and druggists. Dentistry attracts you, as does espionage, military intelligence, the security forces, the Boy Scout movement. Gardening, yet curiously not farming, is attractive to you and many Scorpions make fine market gardeners. Other occupations: insurance brokers, scrap metal dealers, locksmiths, stage musicians, astrologers, psychiatrists, sex therapists, translators, scientists, underground workers – miners, for example, or sewer workers – and tax experts.

Where to live: Scorpions often take up odd sports (like caving – you like the secrecy), so all the areas where your sports can be followed are natural choices (limestone country, in England, for example). You like places like Bavaria, Algeria, Bolivia, Brazil and Budapest, where few tourists go. You like your own special, secret holiday places – the little village in Cornwall or Spain, the Italian mountain village which is especially yours – for a few weeks each year, anyway. You like big cities – because you can be anonymous there. Places to live: Dover, Glossop, Preston, Peterborough, Bath, Liverpool, Stockport, Kew, Bournemouth, Hayling Island, Salford, Southampton, Falmouth. Overseas: Boston, Baltimore, Berlin, Sicily, Catalonia, the Bahamas, Ghent, Brussels, Mainz, Madrid, New Orleans, Paraguay, El Salvador (but wait until things settle down) and Santa Barbara.

SAGITTARIUS (22nd November – 21st December)
You're creative and idealistic, philosophical and ardent. You're set to be a success because you have all the attributes but one – you lack the killer instinct, you won't ever consider hurting someone else to achieve your ends. You will always have real friends and be highly regarded and protected (although you often won't know it). Your choices of occupation are wide: you have the talents to do many things. It's safer for you to consider jobs with some degree of artistic merit, as that suits you better. You make fine ad writers, copy writers, airline personnel (the best flight attendants are

Sagittarian) and animal tenders of one kind or another, from zoo keepers to veterinarians. You are specially good as lawyers, legal clerks, officers of a court or anything related to the legal system. Broadcasting suits you well, and the church is a major calling for you Sagittarians.

Herbs and spices are something you understand – so you can be successful as a cook or chef, as a pharmacist, garden shop proprietor or health food shop owner. Many welfare workers are Sagittarians, as you make fine counsellors. You are wonderful diplomats and representatives of your government, company or special interest group. It's because you are sincere, see the whole picture and have an open mind about helping others achieve their ends, too.

Other occupations that are suited to your talents: anything to do with horses, importing, lecturing, writing, preaching, philanthropy, airline piloting, prophecy, publishing, selling, the fine arts – but as a producer of art, not a dealer. Anything to do with travel: running an agency, being a courier, a holiday salesman.

Where to live: you like an odd mixture of places, and the places on this planet that best suit you Sagittarians are scattered and varied. It's because you really are creatures of the Space Age and you'd be as happy in a colony orbiting a distant star as you are in Cheltenham.

Let's look at the options for earthbound Sagittarians: Alabama, Arabia, Argentina, Australia, Avignon, Belgium, Borneo – for a short visit only – Bradford, Burma, Chile, Cologne, Ecuador, Provence, Hungary, Illinois, Idaho, Mississippi, Naples, Nottingham, Pennsylvania, Portland, Oregon, Zimbabwe, Retford, Ware, Toronto, Rome and Garmisch.

CAPRICORN (22nd December – 19th January)
Position, honour and ambition drive you Capricorns. You are just and cautious, invariably successful, whatever your

occupation and although the world sees you as a somewhat stern and unbending person you have a soft centre. Your occupation must be rewarding in material as well as spiritual ways. Consider these occupations, for which your talents are admirably suited: architect, builder, civil engineer, civil service officer, contractor, anything to do with dealing in precious metals, economist, farmer, anything to do with property, gardener, or anything to do with flowers, plants or greenery. Then there are other options open to you: railways and transportation management, grain and food supplies, leather work, masonry, minerals and their discovery, shaping and marketing, politics, pottery, publishing – anything to do with the printed word, from marketing word processing machinery to producing a small newspaper or news sheet for your social club or organisation – sculpture, osteopathology – anything to do with the human skeleton – time and clock making and anything mechanically-oriented.

Where to live: you should consider the technically-advanced parts of the world. The backwoods are just not for you. New York and London are fine – anywhere you can find electronics, mechanical systems and efficiency. Germany, Switzerland and Austria are splendid. Often you Capricorns are to be found in the capital cities of the world, Washington and Moscow, Rome and Paris. It's just where you gravitate without even knowing quite why. Some other places: Greece, Hesse, Calcutta, Cairo, New Zealand, New England, New Mexico, the South Pacific, Reykjavik, Honolulu, Colchester, Winchester, Saxony, the Vatican. Some successful Capricorns live in places where they can have their comforts and a pleasant climate, like Bermuda, northern California, Florida or the outer islands of the Bahamas.

For you Capricorns generally, however, just where you live isn't as critical to your mental well-being as it is for others of the Zodiac. You'll make money, be successful and self-contained wherever you are – it's your nature.

AQUARIUS (20th January – 19th February)
You are scientists at heart, Aquarians. You're progressive
and adventurous and any kind of new challenge is exciting to
you. You are the frontiers people of the Zodaic, always
seeking new and excitingly different areas to explore,
unconventional and optimistic that over the next horizon will
be the Promised Land. You know that even the Garden of Eden
looked better from a distance, but you are quite prepared to
find out at first hand, then move on to try again. It means that
you need an occupation where constant challenge is a part of
your daily life, where you'll never be in a rut, where you can feel
that the whole planet is yours, not just some cosy corner of it.
You probably wanted to race cars when you were younger –
many Aquarians are still dashing drivers even into old age –
and the sea and travel on its mysterious wastes calls to you in
strong waves of emotion. You make good radio and
television broadcasters, and your inclination to flight means
you also make ornithologists, studying birds, or naturalists
who study the migratory patterns of animals. You're very
cooperative, and are a joiner of groups and societies – until
they pall because they are less changing than you would like.
You make excellent legislators, Members of Parliament,
insurgents and activists in any cause. Electricity and
electronics attract you, as do any kind of dealing with
inventions, from inventing through patenting. You make
excellent instrument designers, manufacturers or dealers,
marvellous mechanics and splendid photographers – because
you constantly search for new approaches to your subjects.
Other occupational areas are: geological survey, oil and oil
industry, physics and chemistry, social and welfare work,
research of almost any kind but especially concerned with
fluids – blood, water, acids, anything to do with telephones
and televisions and finally astrology – because of the
challenge of the sheer size of the Universe and its potential
effects on humankind. It's a mysterious frontier – and that's
its appeal for you.

Where to live: your restless nature means you want to keep moving, as the settled life doesn't really suit your temperament. You like to live in slightly off-beat areas, in desert places like Arizona or Abyssinia or Arabia. (Many Aquarians live and work in the Persian Gulf, where they combine their oil exploration and drilling talents with this desert-dwelling inclination.) But you also enjoy more diverse areas, Brighton and Bremen, Innsbruck and Israel. Anywhere linked to the space age – Cape Kennedy, in Florida, or Huntsville, Alabama or Houston, Texas will delight you. You also enjoy living in places like Sheffield, where the contrast between the city and the open moors above it suit you admirably. Salisbury, Shrewsbury, Exeter, Esher, Richmond, Gloucester, anywhere on the Isle of Man, Oregon, Sweden and Bonn – these are good places for your Aquarian spirit to settle (even if it is only for a shor time).

PISCES (20th February – 20th March)
Yours is the classic water sign, and your nature, changeable, mysterious and able to influence or be influenced easily matches the fluidity of your zodiac sign. For maximum reward, you should seek an occupation that allows your nature full flow and freedom. Acting is one such profession ideally suited to you – so anything with a hint of drama, of let's-pretend about it will do nicely. It might be as a character actor in a stage or television play; it might be as a school teacher leading small children to use their imaginations – it can even be as a dance teacher, helping others to use their bodies and imaginations to temporarily escape everyday routines.

You make very fine teachers, because you are intuitive, sympathetic and sensitive to others. You make excellent animal handlers or trainers, artists, bar-tenders and charity organisers. Chemistry attracts you, and you are often good chemical engineers, pharmacists or researchers for the drug industry. Many Pisceans are spiritualists, clairvoyants, members of religious orders or are somehow closely associated with churches. Fishing, the sea and water generally are attractive to you. You might be a water engineer, or a fisherman, or concerned with canning or distributing seafood. Odd occupations, like divers and frogmen are satisfying to you. You are found happily running service stations, working in mining or quarrying, dealing with hydraulics, canals, reservoirs and rivers. Hospitals attract you, as does work with prisons or young offender rehabilitation. Police work and some aspects of the military – especially the Navy – appeal to you greatly. You make excellent executives – but not top bosses – because you enjoy the responsibility but not the final decision-making.

Where to live: your ideal home would be in a renovated abbey or monastery, by an inlet of the sea, in a remote area. Any Piscean loves to be near water, be it a river, lake, ocean or just a small fishpond in the garden. So coastal towns are happy homes for you – from cities like Southampton to small villages like lovely Mawnan Smith, near Falmouth. North Africa, Southern Asia, almost all of Europe, Brittany, Galicia and Greece are all splendid places for astrological Fish. Lancaster and King's Lynn, Micronesia and Portugal, Jamaica and the West Indies, Harlech and Hartlepool – these too have the right astrological influences for you Pisceans. Parts of Scotland are good for you – Edinburgh, the western Isles and Aberdeen (which happens to be a major fishing port . . .) as well as Grimsby, Fleetwood and Hull – these are all excellent places for your sign.

Chapter Five
The best deal for you

Lewis Carroll

Making a deal is something everyone else seems to do so well – but we never can. We've all had the galling experience of shopping for a car, a coat or a specific item of furniture for weeks and weeks. We find the exact thing, at the right price and boast gently about it the next day to a colleague or a friend. 'But why didn't you tell *me*?' the wretch screams, 'My cousin has that exact thing, for half the price.'

How and when to make deals, what are your best buying habits, whether you should buy new, second hand or downright shabby; whether hire purchase, cash purchase or leasing is the answer for your personality, when to buy and what are your astrologically lucky times to make major purchases – these are all questions we shall look at for your personal star sign in this chapter.

If you are planning a major purchase – a house, car, caravan, holiday or a new wardrobe – you should consider some of the points we raise. We are all affected by the stars' influences and if we buy at a time when our emotional balances are in harmony with the purchase it will be a successful one. We all of us have bought something that we hated the minute we got it home – and few of us have the nerve to return it. This chapter's advice should help reduce the number of such purchasing disasters, and liberate funds for the things that are truly important to you.

And don't forget to consult Appendix I to find your personal lucky numbers to help you with your purchases.

ARIES (21st March – 19th April)
You Ariens are your own worst enemies when it comes to shopping, dealing and buying. You are too impulsive. Try not to shop when you are euphorically happy, or when you are in a rush. It isn't a good idea to dash out from the office at lunchtime to buy a piece of jewellery for your loved one, or clothes for yourself. Give yourself time.

Some things you do get right naturally and without much research, so you can trust your instincts. A holiday, for example, is a major purchase – but you invariably know what you want and you get it. Buying a car is a slightly different matter. If you are buying a new one, check the consumer guides. Do the same for a second hand car – but then spend a few extra pounds and have a mechanic check it over. You have a tendency to fall in love with a given car and drive it away, ignoring expensive faults. Clothing is another danger area – you'll too often be disappointed with something once you get it home. Feel free about taking it back to the shop, remembering of course not to wear it too long first.

Try to buy during the spring clearance sales as it's a good time of year for you and your buying instincts will be at their best. Use your natural Arien sense of adventure to convince the other party that they will be going along on the chance of a lifetime if they can just agree with you – on your terms.

For major purchases, like a car or home furnishings, you'll have to choose between new and used. You aren't generally materialistic and will make sensible decisions based on your own circumstances. For example, you might need a car for your work, and it would be sensible to buy a reliable, comfortable one because you will spend a lot of time in it. But you might not need the prestige of a shiny new model, and will settle for a second hand car of a slightly more expensive make than you would have bought new. It will mean you'll have the comfort but not the initial depreciation burden.

TAURUS (20th April – 21st May)
There is little need to caution you about impulse buying, Taureans. You are a happy, thrifty shopper but you have two areas of potential weakness. You like to indulge your tastebuds and are likely to impulse shop if you find yourself in a gourmet food shop and you have an appreciation for the finer things in life, and will think little of overspending on antiques or works of art you really can't afford.

Avoid the first problem by only shopping for food with a shopping list – and keeping to it. Seeing your weakness for caviar or smoked salmon actually written down week after week will wean you away from overspending on it (although just a moderate amount won't destroy your budget).

Avoiding overspending on art and antiques is a little more difficult. Perhaps you could reach an agreement with your spouse, lover or parent to monitor your art-dealing activities; or limit your purchases to a given monthly amount; or even to restrain yourself by limiting the actual number of such objets d'art you have in the house. If you convince yourself that you can only have this new one if you sell one of your old ones, you'll put your desire to purchase to a real acid test.

Times to buy: you do well at sales times generally, and as you have the self-discipline can buy presents for others months ahead of their birthdays or Christmas. Among your best buys: antiques, because you enjoy them, schooling for your children and home furnishings and books.

GEMINI (22nd May – 20th June)
You airy Geminis will buy when you're happy – to celebrate. You lead a charmed financial life, always on the verge of being

penniless, yet always somehow surviving. You don't follow the rules, you make impulse buys and last-minute buys, you splurge all your savings on gifts. Your budget rarely balances, even though you make sporadic attempts to make it do so, yet everything invariably works out well for you. It's because you live off your wits and can always think yourself out of a tight corner. Follow a few rules, however, and these tight corners will loosen a little, and there will be fewer of them. Buy when you need to, not simply because you want to, and give yourself time to buy – don't rush out an hour before the wedding for a gift, because that way you are certain to overspend.

Certain times of year are good for you to make major purchases: the new year, when January sales are under way; midsummer, when astrological influences on you are at their best and during the Christmas rush, when your keen wits will pick up the tempting bargains that are 'loss leaders' to entice you to buy more.

Clothes are a major item of expenditure for you as you like to be smartly dressed. Consider opening an account with a major store. Cars are another major item on your budget. You enjoy having a fine car, but quickly tire of it. Hiring a car could be the answer for you, because you can easily change it every year or two, with minimum loss, outlay or depreciation.

For business deals, use your innate love of information gathering to get inside knowledge your client or business colleague would not normally expect you to have. The slight shock effect will make you seem even more knowledgeable and could clinch the deal for you very favourably.

Planning savings for you isn't easy but a building society, with its on-demand withdrawal system, might be the best purchase of future security you can make.

CANCER (21st June – 22nd July)

Buy your big purchases when you're feeling insecure,

Cancerians. It's the best pick-you-up you can find for your personality, you'll invariably choose exactly the right things and you'll even find the right price. You make a fierce shopper when you're down in the dumps, so just go with your instincts and save. Try not to buy when you're hurried, when you're preoccupied with a love affair or when you receive unexpected money. Purchases made when you are dashing about invariably are the wrong fit, the wrong colour, size, or somehow reflect the wrong mood for you – and you're moody enough. Things you buy when you're having one of your frequent soulful love affairs also tend to reflect the mood of that moment, and somehow don't seem right the next day.

As for using unexpected largesse to make purchases – retreat into your shell and think it over, then re-think it again. Usually you'll find you don't really need the new purchases and some unexpected debt will come along to eat up much of the windfall. Just store it away for the time being.

Autumn is the best time for you to make household purchases. It could be the onset of winter, the first chills that make you want to get your home snug, warm and inviting – and there is nothing closer to a Crab's heart than his home – but purchases made then, especially of household furniture and soft furnishings, of clothes or of early Christmas gifts are most successful.

When it's time for you to make major purchases, consider hire-purchase for cars. You enjoy the sense of slowly gaining possession of something, and as you tend to take good care of your possessions, the vehicle will still be in excellent condition at the end of the purchase period. Younger Cancerians are happier making their first car purchase outright – they usually don't have a home yet, so the car is a sort of surrogate. They are often mechanically skilled, so an older car if reasonably preserved is a good buy for them.

Tenacity is your forte when it comes to swinging a deal. Be

prepared to keep on bidding, to keep on presenting your case, to continue talking and the person with whom you are dealing will eventually crumble.

Buy insurances on all your household goods, on your life, and against the possibilities of illness or redundancy. You'll feel better for having them and they can also be a way of saving, if you obtain endowment policies. Another investment purchase you will enjoy: antiques, rare coins or stamps. You'll make these buys your hobby, and you can, with shrewd purchases, watch them appreciate considerably, which will add to your enjoyment of them.

LEO (23rd July – 22nd August)
Leos love to make a big, splashy purchase. You are totally at home wandering into the new car showroom and plonking down cash, in fivers, for the shiny new automobile you want. What the impressed salesman doesn't know is that you have employed all your feline cunning and patience to save the cash, painfully, over the past several years. And what you don't recognise is that you are equally liable to give away the car to a relative or friend in a few months' time. You see, you love the grand gesture, and the goods themselves are only a means of making that gesture.

It doesn't do your economic state any good, though. You'll still need a car. So plan a little. You are inclined to open-handedly throw your money about, so protect yourself against it a little. You don't need to be parsimonious – and you never will be, because it isn't in your nature – you just need to think further ahead. The car, for example: lease it. You can't give it away that way. Then put the money you would have spent on it into gilt-edged stocks (Treasury are yielding 133/4% on the 1993's) which can give you up to about 18% gross if you are an average British taxpayer. Get them through the Bonds and Stock office – your local post office has the forms. Then you'll have a tremendous line to chat about at parties – how you've shrewdly got your new car and invested in the country . . .

Some basic advice for you Leos: avoid all impulse buys. You are not good at them generally. Don't buy things when you are deliriously happy – you'll give away too much to an unscrupulous trader. Don't buy too early, either. Christmas presents that you buy in July are likely to be given away, on impulse, to other people, by October.

Do spend on your children's schooling. Private education can be an excellent investment for you as you won't mind the sacrifice and you'll be giving a priceless gift, for life.

When you need to deal with your bank manager for a loan, do dress up in your Leo finest. You'll dazzle him with your stage presence, swing the loan, and being a Leo, probably make firm friends with him, too.

VIRGO (23rd August – 22nd September)

Clever, pennywise virgins know that the more you don't know how to do, the less you have to do. You tend to apply this rule to your financial lives because someone is always likely to step in to help. But the injustice is that when you take over the accounts, matters improve. Use your natural strengths as appraisers to increase your buying power. You have sharp eyes for a bargain. Most times of the year are good for you when you need to buy something. You take full advantage of all clearance sales. You buy at just the right times – snapping up winter clothing at reduced rates in late spring, and saving it; purchasing beachwear in December for next summer's holiday in the Mediterranean. You're smart, organised and conscientious. Where do you go wrong? Simply in your lack of confidence. You feel you haven't any financial sense, that money matters are beyond you.

Two or three suggestions about buying habits: don't buy without checking price, quality and reliability first. If it's a durable item – a washing machine, for example – check on service records of similar machines. The consumer guides will help as will your local repair shop. If you are paying for an extension to your house, ask the builders who submit estimates if they can give you the names of previous customers. A good builder will – and a telephone call to someone who has had work done by him will be useful in giving you some background.

If you are buying clothes, do ensure they fit before you take them. You are inclined to be finicky about colour, fit and cut so be careful.

You are inclined to save up first, buy later. That's good for you, but not so good for other zodiac signs. You tend to decide what you want, then set about getting it, and are unlikely to fritter away a painfully saved amount on something whimsical. Do use your natural Virgo alertness and tact when you are dealing with a merchant, or with the loan officer at the building society.

LIBRA (23rd September – 22nd October)
Artistic Librans like you can make even shopping a matter of grace, style and economy. You plan ahead, you know what you want and you go and get it with maximum efficiency and lack of fuss. You're the sort of shopper who keeps receipts, snips labels to make certain you can match the exact size; has a notebook and pen in your possesion and knows which shops, in which order, to visit for major shopping excursions.

You enjoy buying antiques, books, art works, prints, wine, soft furnishings for your home and gifts for others. You don't enjoy shopping for things like car insurance, clothes, shoes or bank loans. Don't shop for these latter when you are with someone else because you'll feel guilty at trailing them about with you. Try to do some research by telephone first, where possible – you'll save your temper and your feet.

Make domestic purchases during sales times – linens in

January, for example, winter clothes in the spring. You enjoy knowing that you have planned ahead, you'll save money because you bought cheaply (and forestalled inflation, too) and you'll have more and better choices than when everybody else wants the same things at the same time.

Buying security for yourself isn't easy, but small amounts saved regularly will mount up dramatically. If you are an average British tax-payer, you'll get these percentage returns from these savings sources: clearing banks – 11%; (13% on savings accounts, with strings attached like a three month minimum deposit); building societies – up to 15% on term accounts of three years; National Savings Banks – up to 15%; gilt-edged – about 14%; guaranteed income bonds – up to 17% on four year term bonds. Certain of these savings tactics require minimum deposits, so check locally to find out.

Buying a car, boat or caravan? Use your organisational abilities, and find out where you can obtain the cheapest money – as a personal loan from your bank; from your building society or from a hire-purchase company. The difference might seem small, at perhaps a percentage or less – but over several thousand pounds, it can be substantial. And don't try to shop for the money at the last minute, either!

SCORPIO (23rd October – 21st November)
You don't like people to know when you are shopping for something special. You hate to ask friends about whether this kind of car or those sort of holidays are any good. You don't mind doing some basic research at the local library, of course, where nobody knows what you are doing but how do you get that personal knowledge without losing money now and then? Easy, secretive Scorpions. Most durable goods are tested by the excellent consumer organisations, whose reports can be found at the library. Local builders have to be registered, and the local chamber of commerce or town hall will have a log of complaints against tradesmen, so you can

check there. You can of course ask them where they are working at present, and drive by. . . .

Scorpions like you love to hoard things, and frequently buy in bulk because it's cheaper. It can, however, be more expensive. Buy in bulk only when you'll use it all. Waste and spoilage can eat up your apparent savings on a variety of bulk and economy purchases – and you are tying up capital. Check to see if the in-bulk price is really more attractive than smaller amounts.

Take lower running costs into account when you buy durables. More expensive goods can be cheaper if you aren't spending a fortune on keeping them in repair; some clothes with stain repellents or permanent press features might save on dry-cleaning bills, for example. Take into account the company's reputation on its returns policy, as retailers and manufacturers who stand solidly behind what they sell both want and deserve your custom.

Finally, Scorpions, don't buy when you are hurried, unhappy or feeling impulsive.

SAGITTARIUS (22nd November – 21st December)
In the words of the song, Sagittarians: 'You gotta shop around.' Your basic traits of idealism and philosophical acceptance mean that you tend to buy the first thing you see. It's simpler that way, and in an ideal world there wouldn't be any major price differences. Well, there are. Prices do vary, even day to day, on everything from cosmetics to cars. Your best defence is in knowing which stores have built their reputation on dealing in which commodities. You wouldn't go to Woolworth's for a suit but you would go for certain hardware or garden items.

Look out for the real bargains – buy when goods are seasonally reduced. You are intelligent – use that ability to find out which stores put which items on sale, and when they do it. Don't always be fooled by lower prices, though, because sometimes you have to pay more for quality. It can be a false economy to buy cheaper goods because you can lose through spoilage and waste.

Another great help for you slightly impractical Sagittarians when it comes to money is to take counsel. Sound out your family, or your closest friend, on what you are spending. Don't shop hurriedly, do try to save up for major purchases – if not the whole price, at least a major fraction of it. But only on a need-to basis. If you don't need to buy – postpone the purchase.

Astrologically, the spring is your best time for major buys. The spring is also the time when you are most likely to receive an unexpected gift of money.

Be prepared to spend money on insurances, on travel and on education. You enjoy sports, and with a little careful planning can take advantage of end-of-season sales on sporting equipment that you can keep until the next season begins. Look out, too, for used equipment (often for sale just before the new season, as people re-equip).

When you are buying or selling, your strongest point is your genuine interest in other people. Let it out – give it full rein. You'll please the person with whom you are dealing, and will get a better bargain.

For clothing, remember to give an extra bonus point to easy-care fabrics, to stain resistant and crease resistant clothing, permanent press fabrics and so on. They can save on cleaning bills but they usually cost more. Consider the balance – how long will the clothes last and will the savings/extra spendings be worthwhile?

CAPRICORN (22nd December – 19th January)
Of all the signs of the Zodiac, you Capricorns are the best at making a deal. You're tough, practical, determined and unemotional. You can have a passionate attachment to the object you want to buy, but once the price goes beyond what

you coolly, logically think is the right one, you'll drop out of the bidding. This trait means you have tremendous abilities as a businessman or as a negotiator.

You are subject to some weaknesses, though. You'll gladly pay more than the goods are worth to buy something for a loved-one. Try to contain yourself. Remember that you can't buy affection – the people for whom you buy gifts generally do not care if they are expensive or not – they do care that you, busy, business-like you, took the time to shop personally for the gifts.

You should buy gifts early. You can then use your logical brain to truly assess whether they will be totally appropriate and have time to change them if they are not. Astrologically, the best times for you to make major purchases are in the winter, when cool heads and cold blood prevail. Remember to use your lucky numbers to help determine which times of the month are best for making important deals. Winter, too, is a windfall time for you. Unexpected money will come to you then or at least more of it, and more frequently.

Use your buying power to cheer yourself up occasionally, because a gift to yourself can be wonderfully well appreciated. You are a somewhat lonely sign, and even a gift from you to you can be a great morale booster. Important purchases for you include anything for your home but especially furniture, usually made of solid wood, often in light colours. Also important to you is your car. It won't be ostentatious, but it will be a mechanically sound model, perhaps a little older than average – you have no false pride about brand new cars – and will be immaculately kept.

An item many Capricorns enjoy having is a splendid dining table. You like to play a masterful host role, and have enjoyable dinner parties. Often the spiritual centre of your home is the dining room, and a well-set polished oak table gives you a glow far beyond its mere cost. Buy it outright, for cash. You'll always appreciate it, and will always have that strong sense of possession about it. Generally, avoid hire-purchase as you have the willpower to save first, then spend. It will save you money in the long term. Invest in antiques, especially rococco or baroque furniture.

AQUARIUS (20th January – 19th February)
Your best buying gambit is to do it with a friend. A well-prepared Aquarian like you will have a comprehensive list, a map of which stores and where, and a close knowledge of how much to spend and on what. Most Aquarians will have done some comparison shopping before the event and so you will know what you should be paying before you even leave the front door. Alas, an unaccompanied Aquarian will come sadly unstuck. You see, you love people, you love the unconventional and you are easily led astray and away from your purpose. You'll set out to buy a dishwasher and come home with a microwave oven. So, take a friend. Preferably a strong-minded Taurean friend, or a Leo, beside whom all other diversions will pale, or even an organised Virgo or Libra. With your portable conscience in the form of your friend, you can shop in a hurry, when you're depressed or mellow, when you really don't need the goods or even when you go out frankly to indulge an impulse. Your natural wit and quick mind will guide you aright and your friend will make sure you don't give away the shopping money, either.

Spring is your best shopping time, with summer a close second. You will enjoy the stab and grab of the January sales and of the Christmas crush. You can buy new or old, second-hand or cheap and cheerful with impunity. That's all because you invariably will have done your shopping homework. Often you won't even realise you know as much as you do about the product you are setting out to buy – but your voracious reading habits (you scour newspapers from headlines to small advertisements) will have kept you subliminally informed. Buy home furnishings in the spring, buy clothes in the summer, buy silver and jewellery all year round and spend adequately on transportation month by month.

Purchase some security by investing in both a local building society – at about 13% with your money available on demand – or in guaranteed income bonds (which are actually insurance policies) which have a four-year term but yield 17% or so.

If you want to speculate, look to the micro-chip industry or to the booming electronics industry that is about to revolutionise our lives. You forward-looking, scientific Aquarians will feel such an affinity with your investment as you have never felt before.

PISCES (20th February – 20th March)
You and your money are very close friends and like good friends you rarely part. You don't like to spend extravagantly on mere consumer goods – you prefer to make your money work for you, to earn more. You'll spend quite happily on land, on any kind of property which is likely to appreciate but you are reluctant to spend on a shiny new car without some deep, underlying motivation.

There aren't too many good times in the year for you to buy because you don't enjoy buying much anyway. If you have to, the early winter is about the best for you. There are, however, certain in-built astrologically excellent times each month that are highly suited to those born under the sign of the Fish. Investments made between the 8th and the 12th of the month will be sound ones; purchases should be made at the very end of the month, between the 25th and 28th days for major purchases, around the turn of the month for anything else.

You should never buy in haste, neither should you buy on impulse or when you are unhappy. Your intuitive instincts should be given full rein for purchases involving antiques, art or silver (which is your favourite precious metal). Your inherent self-discipline makes you an ideal candidate for hire-purchase agreements.

When you buy clothing, be prepared to spend a little more for 'classic' garments – they won't date or go out of fashion. Keep your monthly charge and credit accounts down to a reasonable figure.

Consider the company with whom you are dealing in the light of its service and returns policy. It can pay you to spend a little more knowing that you have an in-built guarantee of quality – or a new appliance. Use 'pence-off' coupons you can clip from your local newspaper, or have delivered in packets to your home. Buy out-of-season goods, for example, bicycles in January, bathing suits after mid-August. Televisions are cheaper in May and June than at any other time (except in Olympic years), fishing equipment is cheap in October.

Don't be afraid to spend on a holiday, on schooling for your children or on investment-quality antiques. You'll buy some cheap and cheerful things because they are unimportant to you; you'll be happy with a second-hand car for similar reasons. Use your lucky numbers when you set important appointments for deals and close those deals by impressing your client with your intuitive knowledge and sensitivity.

Chapter Six
Business partners

'Joy is a partnership
Grief weeps alone;
Many guests had Cana,
Gethsemane had one.'

Frederic Lawrence Knowles

It is just as important to find the ideal business partner as it is to find the ideal marriage partner, perhaps even more so. Most anxieties, crises, and separations come from lack of money, failure in career, and suspicions and jealousy of the partner. After all, more time is spent with one's business partner than with one's marriage partner. Challenges and confrontations happen every day, and it is only the wise and philosophical person who can handle other people with the subtle manoeuvrings which are readily revealed in their horoscope.

Each business relationship, as each love relationship, is unique, depending on the birthdate of the partners. As in marriage there is no such thing as a bad business partnership, but there are difficult ones – erratic, stubborn, perverse, rambunctious, cranky, wild, and fussy. Yet a partner's idiosyncrasies combined with one's own, can somehow create the magic recipe for success in a particular line of business, where in another line or in another time and place, the two would only experience failure.

But it is vital to look back at failures in business and not be too critical of them; they could have been important stepping-stones which led you to present success. Or if you are going through a restrictive and burdensome time, it could be the pinnacle of success in the future, whether near or far. Remember there are no failures – only lessons learnt.

Sometimes clients will panic when the 'secure' job is suddenly taken away from them, or their partner decides that the time has come to 'divorce'. In 99% of cases they go on to better jobs, newer and exciting partnerships and never regret the changes that gave them so much mental anguish at the time. Many were able to keep a friendly, and then later business, contact with their former partners even though they felt rejected at the time.

Occasionally individuals will hang on to a partnership and business long after it has outlived its use, and by doing so hold themselves back both financially and professionally. This tenacity, often labelled loyalty, is a weakness, allied to the fear of leaving home.

There is a strong trend in astrology for certain signs to be attracted. There are the teacher-student attractions, the lovers, the husbands and wives, the competitors and rivals, the doctor and the patient, the lawyer and the client, and most important, the business partnership, whether equal partners, or the boss-employee combination. Certain signs are better for one rule, others for other functions.

It is also good to remember, and many of you would have experienced this already, that in business as well as in love partnerships *you don't have to be happy all the time*. Remember, if it never rained we would have no grass, plants, flowers and trees. It is the same in business. You must think only of what is the goal of the company and the relationship, not worry about the nitty-gritty chores and obstacles of every day living.

Each sign of the zodiac is either fire (Aries, Leo, Sagittarius), air (Gemini, Libra, Aquarius), earth (Taurus, Virgo, Capricorn), or water (Cancer, Scorpio, Pisces), and people born under these signs conform to these four elements.

The fire signs are flamboyant, extrovert, outrageous and daring, these are the showmen and women of the zodiac.

The air signs are mentally creative and agile, witty and very hard to hold down; they are also escapists who don't want to be tied down by any heavy committment.

The earth signs, as their name suggests, are down to earth and practical – often boringly so – but good at work which requires precision and accuracy.

The water signs are extremely emotional, prone to generosity and self-sacrifice; they think of everyone as part of their family, and act from the heart rather than from the bank-book.

Partners in the same grouping would be natural partners for they would behave and see things in the same way, yet they could miss an important ingredient by lacking the qualities of other elements. 'Cross-pollinating' can work magic and evolve a team whose ideas far surpass the small-time ambitions thought so important at the beginning.

Fire signs go well with air signs; fire needs air to live, and while too much fire can make a lot of 'hot air' and too much air can put out the fire, this combination can achieve great things.

Water signs mix well with earth signs, especially when you consider that too much earth can dry up the water, too much water can make mud, but the right amount of each can make flowers grow.

Some mixtures, however, are difficult and never actually get it together to form a partnership unless there are other planetary forces in the horoscope chart which make it possible. Fire is hard to mix with earth and water as they would dampen the spirit and reduce the power of the 'spark'. You could of course get a lot of steam from a fire and water combination, and if channelled properly put that steam into powerful action. Likewise air, earth and water don't mix well; air can give life to earth if no water is around, but air and water create fog, mist and rain.

Probably the most important attitude to have is that in business, as in love, all relationships are possible. It is just that some are better than others, after all, 'if two partners continually agree, one is unnecessary'.

ARIES AS PARTNER
BEST BETS: Aries are excellent partners for other Aries, Leos and Sagittarians, as all have a daring gambling streak, unconventionally trying to shock the rest of the big business world out of their restrictive ruts. As partners they see things on a grand scale and run their lives on a basically military routine with the Aries General, the Leo King and the Sagittarian Bishop, heading up the strategic command. Virgo and Libra are also natural partners, Virgo lends a more down to earth attitude and takes on the financial responsibilities of the team; and Libra, being the opposite sign to Aries, lends calm, patience and control and helps keep Aries out of impulsive legal hassles.

EXPANSION: It is important that the partner realises right from the beginning the need for Aries to be continually expanding and testing new ideas. But someone must hang on to the purse strings. A wise Aries will appoint a strict business manager or book-keeper to handle this. Beware of buying new gadgets and furniture for the business on impulse, that will never be used.

EVERYDAY EXPENSES: Aries must sit down and work out a plan of attack; a plan of income and expenditure, to help control reckless spending. Even though practical and logical at the time, in retrospect Aries tends to waste money. The partner cannot totally control this urge, but by going over accounts can get the full support of Aries. Habits can be changed and new disciplines can become new habits.

FINANCIAL CRISIS: Everyday will seem like a financial crisis to Aries. There is never enough money for the grand scale schemes and when there is a large amount floating around, it will soon be used up. However, at times of true money crises Aries will become self-disciplined and frugal until things are worked out better. It is important that the partner is open and honest about all financial situations. Aries will quickly adapt to what is required.

POLICY DECISIONS: Always a leader, Aries will want to be involved with the final decisions and changes made by the company. However, like the good Generals that they are, they can delegate authority and listen to advice. But it is still difficult for them not to want to make a final judgement – uneducated or not.

OTHER PARTNERS: Aries will in their lifetime work with every sign of the zodiac, their relationship being unique in each case.

Aries-Aries: A dynamic duo, destined to become impressarios and millionaires.

Aries-Taurus: Excellent business team financially; Taurus may slow down Aries.

Aries-Gemini: Can get bogged down with too much discussion, and wordy paper work.

Aries-Cancer: Too many business lunches, not enough business meetings.

Aries-Leo: Good for speculative ventures, especially show-business deals.

Aries-Virgo: Excellent business team, very practical, but too many lists and charts.

Aries-Libra: Libran's indecisiveness makes this otherwise good team nervous.

Aries-Scorpio: Both ambitious, but Scorpio is too secretive, and Aries too open.

Aries-Sagittarius: Daring combination. Any big gamble is sure to pay off eventually.

Aries-Capricorn: A difficult partnership. Capricorn will be a wet blanket!

Aries-Aquarius: Exciting, but both will be bossy and think they know it all.

Aries-Pisces: A feeling of confusion by Pisces will slow down Aries enthusiasm.

TAURUS AS PARTNER

BEST BETS: Taurus combines well with Virgo, Capricorn and fellow Taureans, all being exceptionally practical, shrewd and hard working. They lack the lustre and excitement of other signs but they do come up with the goods. This team is sure to make money. They will do it quietly and diligently. These are the traditional fraternal partners, socially the pillars of society – the Virgo Teacher, the Capricorn Politician, and the Taurus Banker, all wanting to improve their community economically. Scorpio and Cancer make excellent partners too, Scorpios being philanthropic as well as very ambitious for themselves and also for their associates. Cancer's concern over the well-being of their family and interest in institutions and organisations, help Taurus make a success with hotels, restaurants, super-markets and shopping developments.

EXPANSION: Taureans need dynamic partners to boost their talents and to encourage them to take chances. There is a conservative approach to speculation, but with the affection and respect of a daring and proven successful partner, they can become great merchant bankers, stockbrokers and backers of large industrial projects. The low profile preferred by Taurus can soon disappear, and the star quality will shine through one big success after another.

EVERYDAY EXPENSES: In partnership Taurus will watch every penny and want a proper cashier's receipt for every business lunch and travelling expense. Yet they will lavishly entertain for an obscure business associate or send expensive flowers to the sick wife of one of the workers. Partners, while encouraging this admirable trait, should stop them spending so much of the company's time checking, double checking and being too analytical when there are more important jobs to be done.

FINANCIAL CRISIS: Rarely will Taureans be in a position where a crisis will suddenly occur. They plan so far in advance that they can tell when things may go wrong. Let them handle it themselves with encouragement and advice. Creditors, banks and business associates all appreciate the simple approach Taureans have to tackling crises and their straightforward solutions.

POLICY DECISIONS: Listen to the Taurus partner recite the by-laws and the local government restrictions carefully and abide by them. But don't look to them for innovative policy changes that will turn the company from a successful Victorian business into a major modern twenty-first century money maker.

OTHER PARTNERS: Taurus will be very discriminating when choosing a partner yet all signs are possible for different reasons.

Taurus-Aries: Aries will give the touch of magic that will make great success.

Taurus-Taurus: Slow, methodical but excellent team. Big money makers in securities

Taurus-Gemini: Gemini's mercurial nature will make Taurus nervous and insecure.

Taurus-Cancer: Excellent for large conglomerates and in planning industrial estates.

Taurus-Leo: Both very stubborn, but Leo can add the glitter that Taurus needs.

Taurus-Virgo: Perfect, both hard working, make a winning team, but lacks excitement.

Taurus-Libra: A successful combination for business in the fine arts and fashion.

Taurus-Scorpio: Scorpio's methods may worry Taurus, but success once convinced.

Taurus-Sagittarius: Difficult, freedom loving Sagittarius will gamble too much.

Taurus-Capricorn: Excellent, especially for large international ventures.

Taurus-Aquarius: Difficulties through Aquarius's impulsive and stubborn behaviour.

Taurus-Pisces: Good for work connected with medical care, as both charitable.

GEMINI AS PARTNER

BEST BETS: Geminis readily choose other air signs Libra and Aquarius, as well as fellow Geminis as partners, for they all enjoy freedom of personality, even though they love to work with others. While their ideas may seem disorganised to the outside world, their minds are full of interesting data. The Gemini Negotiator, the Libra Diplomat and the Aquarian Scholar have a wealth of information about everything, that channelled into the marketable outlet, could make millions. Sagittarius and Aries have enough drive and gambling instinct to work as ideal partners with Geminis too. The wit and humour of Gemini and Sagittarius combines to present the world with some crazy business schemes that pay off. And Aries will push Gemini into action by sheer strength of character.

EXPANSION: It is more a case of stopping Gemini from going off in too many directions, than looking for new outlets for their talents and business acumen. Their curiosity and need to know about everything, plus an insatiable appetite for books, magazines and newspapers, has their minds going in many directions at one time. It is important to allow them more than one project as Geminis are capable of handling more than one thing at a time – but they should be discouraged from spreading themselves too thin.

EVERYDAY EXPENSES: More money will be spent on telephone calls and postage than anything else. Of course they will be discussing business, but as a partner you must put a time limit on long distance and local telephone calls. They just love to chat. They will probably do very well in selling and making money on the telephone too, so use your own judgement if the overly long conversation will bring in money, or just add to your already excessive phone bill. Naturally subscriptions to all magazines, book clubs and other mail order items, may appear on the company account, and *you* may not read any of them. Discuss these expensive miscellaneous items at the beginning of your relationship.

FINANCIAL CRISIS: Geminis do not cope well with any crises at all, whether financial, romantic or domestic. However they are excellent sympathisers when it comes to other people's problems. At times of major difficulty you may find that Gemini flies off to relax on the beach at a holiday resort. They are escapists. You must handle it all.

POLICY DECISIONS: New ideas and suggestions come regularly and brilliantly. They love to make joint decisions and will discuss new changes and additions with you supportively. They are not competitors. Make all your decisions together, if you can!

OTHER PARTNERS: Gemini is such a friendly sign and can get on with all other signs, but this isn't always a good thing, it can be nerve-wracking.

Gemini-Aries: An aggressive team, more action needed, cut down on all the talk.

Gemini-Taurus: Difficult, but Taurus can help keep Gemini more down-to-earth.

Gemini-Gemini: Excellent with fingers in many business enterprises in the world.

Gemini-Cancer: Unusual, Cancer needs more security than Gemini can really offer.

Gemini-Leo: Good, Leo will love to promote and encourage Gemini's ingenuity.

Gemini-Virgo: Both mercurial, detailed and hardworking. Virgo will add system.

Gemini-Libra: A great team capable of turning out beautiful work and ideas.

Gemini-Scorpio: Both being generous and ambitious they will support each other.

Gemini-Sagittarius: Wonderful and fun. They will take more chances and win often.

Gemini-Capricorn: Boring duo, but good for working in research or publishing.

Gemini-Aquarius: Incredible success once they decide on a business-like direction.

Gemini-Pisces: Neither would ever really know what the other was up to – a weak team.

CANCER AS PARTNER

BEST BETS: Cancer's best partners are other Cancers, Scorpios and Pisces. Emotionally they are right for each other and will work together at the same sensitivity level. They care for each other, their workers and their business associates. The Cancer Parent, the Scorpio Philanthropist and the Pisces Healer work to improve mankind and as partners succeed in any and every business involving the general public. Virgo and Capricorn make perfect business partners too. They add practicality and will reduce the amount of money Cancer donates to charitable situations whether at home or outside. Virgo will help Cancer keep track of every business detail instead of losing them. Capricorn, while being a strict disciplinarian will bring out the best skills and talents by demanding a high performance, as this means money.

EXPANSION: Cancers automatically keep adding people and business ventures to their lives without eliminating any. They love to include everyone in their 'family' and should any member have a good business idea they may back it. As a partner it is important to remember that you are now legally committed to Cancer's whole family, friends, neighbours and other business associates.

EVERYDAY EXPENSES: Feeding everyone is the biggest expense. Lunches, dinners, drinks to woo the out-of-town buyer. Sandwiches, cakes and coffee for all the help twice a day. And the annual staff party or dinner, plus the picnics. Visiting relatives and old school friends may be feeding off the office entertainment budget. Other more important expenses will be left to you.

FINANCIAL CRISIS: Cancers know just how to handle any crisis being the paternal or maternal member of the team.

They have a calming influence on everyone and will protect the entire staff and their families, before allowing any drastic action to close them down, force lay-offs of employees, or jeopardise a partnership. They are too emotional to make quick, cruel financial decisions. Partners are left to do that.

POLICY DECISIONS: Cancers would never forgive their partner if they were left out of any new policy changes. After all it is the family. In many instances the whole company may be called in to help decide certain actions, voting democratically, even against the wishes or feelings of the bosses. It is very important to keep everyone happy and to show fairness and consideration. Then no one can blame any particular individual for any unpopular decisions.

OTHER PARTNERS: Cancers will cherish their partners, no matter what their sign, but can do it with so much affection that they smother and frighten away less emotional colleagues.

Cancer-Aries: Aries would rebel, the emotions and changing moods counter-productive.

Cancer-Taurus: Their mutual interests in big business and the community pay off.

Cancer-Gemini: Not very easy, Gemini's travels will worry Cancer, but pay off well.

Cancer-Cancer: Excellent, they will expand rapidly, and share the same moods.

Cancer-Leo: Should be fun. Leo will add lots of glamorous ideas, and profit.

Cancer-Virgo: A good working team. Each willing to devote time to each other.

Cancer-Libra: Difficult. Libra may be selfish in the goals of the company.

Cancer-Scorpio: Wonderful. Both stick to their goals, making for predictable success.

Cancer-Sagittarius: Two totally different attitudes could be a challenge.

Cancer-Capricorn: Ideal team, opposite points of view make for a big success.
Cancer-Aquarius: Freedom is necessary for Aquarius, Cancer could be too suffocating.
Cancer-Pisces: Perfect working relationship, destined for big rewards and success.

LEO AS PARTNER

BEST BETS: Leos work wonderfully with the other fire signs Aries and Sagittarius and naturally with fellow Leos. They all love the flamboyant nature of big business and speculation. The Aries Commander-in-Chief, the Leo Royal Monarch, and the Sagittarius Gambler control much of the big business that goes on in the world today. Aquarius and Gemini are also good partners for them. Aquarians, the walking encyclopedias of the zodiac, have all the knowledge and abilities that Leo can channel into a fortune. Gemini can best express the way Leo feels, thinks and wants to appear before the public.

EXPANSION: Leos would hardly be considered the Kings of the zodiac (or Queens, of course) if they were not always looking for new territories to conquer. But it must be exciting and challenging, nothing humdrum or routine for them. Preferably they want businesses that have class, nice surroundings, a touch of showbusiness and the possibility to make lots of money. Wealth is a big attraction, more for the use of it for their many extravagant pleasures than to hoard or invest.

EVERYDAY EXPENSES: This is where Leos must be watched carefully and guided. They like the best of everything, the best restaurants, the best wines, the best quality paper for office use, the best designed furniture and the best-looking secretary (whether she can type or not). Looks are more important than the practicalities. They are overly generous and tip excessively. It is the partner's money they are spending as well as their own, so a hint should be dropped early in the arrangement, or written into the contract, who is going to pay for what . . . and how much.

FINANCIAL CRISIS: Just being a Leo is crisis enough. However, somehow a real crisis never turns up. There may be warnings of it, or threats of it, and there may be warrants and lawsuits pending, but miraculously Leos are able to wave the magic wand and obtain the money they need to get their business out of trouble. They know the right people, and the right way of approaching them, and even their bank-managers see them as stars. But the partner mustn't allow a crisis to go on too long so that Leos can demonstrate this trick, one day it could be too late.

POLICY DECISIONS: Leos make them. That's it, nothing more. The partner can kid themselves that they made the suggestion or that it was a joint decision, but in their hearts they know that if Leos want to do it, they do it and vice versa. In most cases it's best to go along with it.

OTHER PARTNERS: Leos don't take much notice of who their partners are, they are usually subservient, or willing to do their bidding, or so they think!

Leo-Aries: Good partners, ideal for trying new ventures, especially entertainment.

Leo-Taurus: Tough team. They are just as hard on themselves as their customers.

Leo-Gemini: Great fun. Gemini knows how to keep Leo amused, and make money too.

Leo-Cancer: A nice sensitive relationship, ups and downs due to Cancer's moods.

Leo-Leo: Two show-offs fighting for the limelight, they need a financial advisor.

Leo-Virgo: Success if Virgo allowed to work away without being 'ruled' by Leo.

Leo-Libra: Good team, but both would want to get the credit. Libra dislikes sharing.

Leo-Scorpio: Difficult, but can make it if they have a big mutual project ahead.

Leo-Sagittarius: Excellent, any risks taken by these two will be lucky and pay off.
Leo-Capricorn: A winning combination, Capricorn may be planning to take over.
Leo-Aquarius: Good working team, together they have the know-how to do anything.
Leo-Pisces: Too many emotional dramas by Pisces, will get Leo off the money track.

VIRGO AS PARTNER

BEST BETS: Virgos love to work with other Virgos, as well as Taureans and Capricorns. They all understand each other's motivation, they are all frank, businesslike and practical and they don't allow any of the emotions, dramas and fantasies of the other signs to interfere with their work. They make good partners for Pisces and Cancer and will get into professions and business associated with the medical, educational and sociological fields. The Virgo Professor, the Taurus Financier, and the Capricorn Union Leader take pride in working for the rights of their fellow men and women, politically and financially.

EXPANSION: It is very unlikely that Virgos will initiate expansion on their own. They need a fiery, aggressive person to give them the boost they need in order to let their light shine. They have great abilities and talents which can remain hidden unless a partner unleashes them. As most Virgo skills are practical and useful in business there should be no fear of investing money and time in them.

EVERYDAY EXPENSES: Virgos have stationery fetishes, they just cannot go past an office supply store without buying something. Just check the supply room. The partner will find enough stationery and office equipment for the next ten years! They will cut back on their lunches, dinners and transport expenses and waste money on unnecessary gadgets and supplies.

FINANCIAL CRISIS: Virgos have the answer to handling every crisis. They make a list of the details, make a plan of payment and collection, and they will present it to the creditors, bank managers and other business associates in such an efficiently laid-out manner, that the problem is immediately solved, and everyone following the plan will be satisfied. They can, however, spend too much time after the fact, checking on details. Let someone else do the follow up.

POLICY DECISIONS: Tell partner Virgo what you want and Virgo will put it in the exact legal terminology, phrase it diplomatically, and come up with brilliant ideas to save the company money. They are time study experts, capable of creating efficient, new systems and reducing overheads. But they have to be asked, told or bullied into it, depending on their individual character. Even though they may be one of the bosses they behave (and enjoy doing so) like a servant to their partners.

OTHER PARTNERS: Virgos will work like Trojans for their partners. But they dislike being bossed or thought of as servile.

Virgo-Aries: Excellent, Aries has the right amount of aggression and ability.

Virgo-Taurus: A hard working duo, willing to work long hours to attain goals.

Virgo-Gemini: A good team, but Gemini needs to learn discipline, and Virgo humour.

Virgo-Cancer: A devoted couple, they produce successful businesses and happy workers.

Virgo-Leo: Leo will add style and glamour, but must watch taking over the show.

Virgo-Virgo: Wonderful, both willing to do everything necessary for success.

Virgo-Libra: Difficult, Libra can be too demanding and not serious enough.

Virgo-Scorpio: A good working relationship, Scorpio will make sure Virgo succeeds.

Virgo-Sagittarius: Unusual, Sagittarius too unpredictable to stick to routine.
Virgo-Capricorn: Perfect, Capricorn has the leadership, Virgo the loyalty.
Virgo-Aquarius: Not bad, but Aquarius tends to want to boss Virgo around too much.
Virgo-Pisces: Good, Pisces will be devoted, and will follow Virgo's plans.

LIBRA AS PARTNER

BEST BETS: Libra should chose another air sign – Gemini, Aquarius or fellow Libra for a partner. They all respect freedom of the mind, hate restrictions in working conditions, and are generally able to look objectively at problems. Their goals tend to be fantasies and dreams, and they have the ability to make these dreams come true in practical and financially successful ways. The Libran Artist, The Gemini Communicator, and the Aquarian Hippy combine to make life exciting and fulfilling. Aries and Sagittarius are other ideal partners for Libra, being daring and spontaneous. Aries won't allow Libra to spend too much time making decisions, and Sagittarius forces the nervous Libra to take a chance, win or lose.

EXPANSION: You cannot leave Librans to make their own decisions. If there is a choice, they will spend hours considering the various reasons for doing one or the other. They are simply indecisive, even when they know what they really want. They will be delighted to follow the partner's lead, yet they can bring style and beauty to any project, building or environment – if you tell them what you would like.

EVERYDAY EXPENSES: They spend a lot of time writing thank-you letters and phoning friends. It is nice to have a born diplomat on the team, and know that they will solve problems but they do go overboard with the niceties of daily living. Tell them it isn't necessary to send flowers, bottles of Scotch, and other gifts to the hotel rooms of visiting business colleagues, unless you both decide it will help make a sale or help the business. Sometimes it can backfire.

FINANCIAL CRISIS: This can make Libra almost suicidal. They cannot stand anything to be off-balance, especially the bank account. The partner must work out a solution first before presenting the problem, and then it should be approached from a positive point of view. Librans must be kept calm in any crisis. They take everything so personally and may blame themselves for any financial losses. A good partner will have learnt early in the relationship that this is the case, and will take charge accordingly.

POLICY DECISIONS: Both Libra and the partner should discuss this, but never let Libra have a choice. The wonderful qualities of Libra enable them to say things and word them in such a way that they are not offensive. Let Libra do the talking. The partner should make the final decision having heard Libra's point of view.

OTHER PARTNERS: Libra is a wonderful partner to have, whatever your sign; they are easy to get along with, and easy to sway. Yet they do have a power complex.

Libra-Aries: A good team. Aries will help force Libra into action with goals.

Libra-Taurus: Both artistic and make ideal partners. Taurus will help make money.

Libra-Gemini: Ideas and creativity come first. Then investors are easy to find.

Libra-Cancer: Cancer will be devoted to Libra, but they will not work well together.

Libra-Leo: Leo will help get both into the public eye. This team has taste.

Libra-Virgo: Not a good team. Libra will be spoilt by Virgo, and won't appreciate it.

Libra-Libra: Good in working together, but difficult making joint decisions.

Libra-Scorpio: Scorpio will make Libra more successful with aggressive actions.
Libra-Sagittarius: Fun and adventurous. Gambles pay off. A courageous team.
Libra-Capricorn: Restrictive, Capricorn will discourage Libra's artistic goals.
Libra-Aquarius: Excellent, Aquarius's computer mind combines with Libra's style.
Libra-Pisces: Weak relationship, both too indecisive to get much accomplished.

SCORPIO AS PARTNER

BEST BETS: Scorpio is ideal for partnerships with other water signs Cancer and Pisces, and always with other Scorpios. Scorpio being the strongest of the three brings out verve and passion in the other less demonstrative partners. The Scorpio Spy, the Cancer Psychic and Pisces Spiritualist combine to make a formidable team, able to call upon all the tricks of the trade to make their business venture a memorable success. Taurus and Capricorn also make wonderful working partners, bring a touch of big business class with them, and the investors to go with it. Taurus may be a little square at times but makes a wonderful front man for Scorpio's nefarious activities! Capricorn knows just the person in government circles to help get a license or development grant.

EXPANSION: Yes, there will be plenty of expansion going on, even though the partner may not see it with his own eyes. The partner must be strict with them and make sure that everything is done legally, even though secretly. However, the partner will never be sure of all that is going on. Scorpio must watch the achievement obsession – many times they achieve a major goal only to find out that they don't want it once they have got it. They tend to do this over and over again. This leaves them always restless for a new goal.

EVERYDAY EXPENSES: Scorpios love to spend. They love to see beauty and fine craftsmenship around them, and therefore spend more than necessary on the office decorations and equipment. They are generous with friends and business colleagues, and philanthropic, donating to nearly all local charities and giving hand-outs to beggars on the streets. These admirable qualities are fine if the budget allows and can be used for tax-deductions too. But set rules early about petty cash, and purchasing individually for the company. Partners should keep an eye on Scorpio. One talent that should be encouraged is their great ability in bargaining with sales people. They can get things for you cheap. And they are extremely honest – all savings are put back into the company.

FINANCIAL CRISIS: They love it. The drama, the emotion, the scandal, the conflict and the legalities, yet they usually get out of it easily. Partners should not allow them to handle all the negotiations but make a mutually agreed plan of attack and keep to it. Otherwise people may think that there are underhanded dealings going on when there aren't – it is just Scorpio's suspicious behaviour.

POLICY DECISIONS: Scorpios have the ability to see where changes need to be made and precisely when to make them. Joint decisions must be made nevertheless and a good partner will allow Scorpios to have their say and consider the suggestions wise, ambitious and timely. Check with the company lawyer if any idea sound illegal. They probably aren't but Scorpio's presentation of them might make them appear so.

OTHER PARTNERS: Scorpio is a difficult partner, even at the best of times, but everyone should have at least one Scorpio in their lives, they get things done.

Scorpio-Aries: Much conflict of interests, but can fight together for a cause.

Scorpio-Taurus: Taurus adds dignity and prestige to Scorpio's unusual schemes.

Scorpio-Gemini: Gemini will help publicise the partnership and get good support.
Scorpio-Cancer: A winning team, both tenacious and won't give in till they win.
Scorpio-Leo: A difficult combination, but if ambitious enough will make a million.
Scorpio-Virgo: Virgo will happily do all the nitty-gritty to make company succeed.
Scorpio-Libra: Libra will aggravate Scorpio, but can be a good trouble-shooter.
Scorpio-Scorpio: A power packed team. Nothing is impossible for them to attain.
Scorpio-Sagittarius: There will be more fights than business. Little in common.
Scorpio-Capricorn: A great partnership, both seek power and help each other get it.
Scorpio-Aquarius: Difficult unless they are willing to compromise their strong ideas.
Scorpio-Pisces: Excellent, Pisces' loyalty and encouragement makes it easy work.

SAGITTARIUS AS PARTNER

BEST BETS: Sagittarians make excellent partners for Aries, Leos, and other Sagittarians. All being fire signs they complement each other well in style, attitudes and image. Basically all have a similar sense of humour and like life, work and money making to be fun as well as rewarding. Sagittarius' natural attraction to risks, chances and gambles requires Leo's flamboyance, and Aries' determination to achieve goals. The Sagittarius Optimist, the Aries Initiator and the Leo Star all have the ability to make a success of anything they do, especially as a team. Gemini and Aquarius are other good possible partners as they both love details and how to make a successful business. Sagittarius alone would be too impatient to check up on all the major details and legalities.

EXPANSION: Sagittarius naturally loves to explore, but they don't want to take on too many responsibilities. When they do expand it is usually to travel to other cities and countries. As a partner it would be wise to consider and encourage geographical growth, as long as there is another partner or helper to get the nitty-gritty done.

EVERYDAY EXPENSES: These can be enormous as Sagittarius is impulsive and generous, and likes the best of everything. They like the best stationery and office surroundings; they dress casually but expensively and travel in the finest limousines. Travel is the biggest expense and naturally this includes airline tickets, hotels, lunches, dinners and drinks, theatre tickets and gifts for business associates. Much petty cash goes as charitable hand-outs to friends, bums and strangers who happen to cross their paths and need money. And if the Sagittarian likes a gamble, it may have to be put down as a regular loss under 'miscellaneous expenses'.

FINANCIAL CRISIS: If there is one, Sagittarius doesn't notice. As partners they keep a wonderful sense of balance during a crisis, are capable of making witty remarks at board meetings to clear the tension, and are more likely to shrug their shoulders to demonstrate that these situations are normal in business. However, they are liable to want to put more time and money into saving the situation than the crisis warrants, and should be discouraged unless all agree that this would be the best move in the long run.

POLICY DECISIONS: Sagittarians are blunt and frank and will say exactly what is on their minds – and kick themselves later for saying it. The partner must keep an eye on what Sagittarius is saying or doing and take the appropriate diplomatic action. Remember, however, that they could be perfectly right in what they say.

OTHER PARTNERS: Sagittarius doesn't particularly like to be tied down to anyone, even in business; they realise, however, that a partner gives them freedom.

Sagittarius-Aries: Exciting team, can accomplish much with their daring schemes.

Sagittarius-Taurus: Taurus can help control the purse strings, thereby making profit.

Sagittarius-Gemini: Excellent. Gemini has great ideas that Sagittarius will back.

Sagittarius-Cancer: Good, as Cancer will look after the business when Sagittarius travels.

Sagittarius-Leo: Very good. Luck in all entertainment and outlandish enterprises.

Sagittarius-Virgo: Virgo will make sure Sagittarius is organised – a good team.

Sagittarius-Libra: Enjoyable working collaboration. Creatively good partners.

Sagittarius-Scorpio: Difficult. Scorpio is too secret, creating unfounded worries.

Sagittarius-Sagittarius: Good, very unconventional and winning combination, if risks are to be taken.

Sagittarius-Capricorn: Not easy, unless Capricorn willing to take over the work.

Sagittarius-Aquarius: Aquarius knows exactly how to market Sagittarius' talents.

Sagittarius-Pisces: Difficult. Pisces needs to work devotedly next to partner.

CAPRICORN AS PARTNER

BEST BETS: Capricorn is ideal working with Taurus, Virgo and other Capricorns. These earth signs have a knack of knowing how to turn a loss into a profit. They are capable of instantly eliminating any extravagant overheads, as they hate to waste money. They don't cling on to the past, once a thing is over it is over. Cancer and Pisces work well with Capricorn as they won't answer back and will happily do as they are told. The Virgo Statistician, the Taurus Specialist and Capricorn

Industrialist can accomplish more in partnership than most other combinations.

EXPANSION: Capricorns expand by buying out their partners, or taking over their boss's company when they go broke. So beware and don't allow them to be totally in control of the accounts, or too friendly with the accountant or lawyer, there may be a conspiracy. As a team they are shrewd, too, so once the partner has assured himself that it isn't his scalp that the Capricorn is after, then together they can hunt someone else's.

EVERYDAY EXPENSES: Capricorns love expensive restaurants and the best wines which will 'eat' into the entertainment account. The partner may be invited along to add salt to the wounds and will have to sit through the extravagant ordeal. A limit should be agreed upon for such occasions. Professional magazines and journals start to build up a hefty bill and Capricorns' desire to have everything checked by a lawyer as well as an accountant adds unwarranted sums of wasted money. Yet they will reprimand office workers for throwing away a paper clip.

FINANCIAL CRISIS: When it happens they are first to say 'I told you so', and will start to chop off heads. They can never be blamed for the problem, they will have many excuses, and many other suspects to accuse. Channel their analytical talents into finding the real cause. They have wonderful systems for handling all situations which prevents them from feeling guilty and blaming themselves. They can be heavy to have around.

POLICY DECISIONS: Most of the time Capricorn will want to make them; the partners should make sure that he types suggestions down well in advance for the Capricorn to read and consider. They don't think broadly and are impatient at policy meetings and can be combative if they think their authority is being questioned or their ideas not respected.

OTHER PARTNERS: Capricorn is a difficult partner to get along with, they tend to be bossy, but they are one of the best for making great business successes.

Capricorn-Aries: Difficult. Too much time spent working against each other.

Capricorn-Taurus: Excellent. Big business activities will make a lot of profit.

Capricorn-Gemini: Gemini can supply the information, Capricorn can market it.

Capricorn-Cancer: Good. Cancer will ensure the other workers' loyalty.

Capricorn-Leo: A great combination, having much flair and determination to win.

Capricorn-Virgo: Capricorn needs a Virgo partner to make sure details are done.

Capricorn-Libra: Difficult. Libra's indecisiveness will make them impatient.

Capricorn-Scorpio: A powerful combination. Both have a great driving force.

Capricorn-Sagittarius: Difficult. Sagittarius too restless and can't be bullied.

Capricorn-Capricorn: Good. Both hard workers and have definite goals – will make money.

Capricorn-Aquarius: Unusual. Aquarius equally opinionated, will be hard to change.

Capricorn-Pisces: Good. Pisces will do everything to make the team a success.

AQUARIUS AS PARTNER

BEST BETS: Aquarians make excellent partners for other air signs Libra and Gemini and, of course, work well with other Aquarians too. Brilliant and original in their outlook and ideas they spark off their partners and come up with money-making projects. The Aquarius Reformer, the Gemini Thinker, and the Libra Creator always produce ideas that will better mankind, at the same time lining their wallets. They are givers, but work on the theory that the more they make the more they can give away. Leo and Aries work well with Aquarius. Leo being a show-off will soon publicly put into action their mutual projects with good taste, glamour and attractive packaging. Aries just as dynamically will stop Aquarius traditionally procrastinating and get on with it, looking out for the next plan while promoting the present one.

EXPANSION: Aquarians spread themselves in every direction. They are interested in whatever is going on at the moment to make some quick money. They do not discriminate and will get into things that they don't particularly like just for the simple reason that it was happening at that particular moment in time. Partners can go crazy keeping track, and should allow Aquarius to have many of these involvements, so long as it doesn't involve them financially or legally. It can take time away from the main business, but that is normal in any case, and the partner should be used to it.

EVERYDAY EXPENSES: There will be lots of these as there are always new reference materials needed, new gadgets for the office, and electrical equipment and computers are the biggest weakness. Phone bills will be high, and there may be resentment on the part of the partner over social, charitable and other extra-curricular activities that eventually get out of hand.

FINANCIAL CRISIS: At least Aquarius will know all the details and be able to answer precisely any delicate or difficult questions about a crisis. Fairly practical and calm, they are confident that they can get through any major critical situation on their wits and their knowledge, using their inventive brain and friendly personality. Partners should beware that they don't feel exploited by Aquarius, generally they are not materialistic, but their eccentric and unconventional behaviour can seem suspicious.

POLICY DECISIONS: They have opinions about everything, and tend to follow fads inhibiting an expansive partner who wants to get on and make money, lots of it. As know-it-alls they will want to force their latest crazy notion on to an already successful business which could jeopardise the credibility of the enterprise. Their policies are humanitarian, altruistic and selfless which is fine for the receiver but very difficult for the partner, who is probably more materialistic and more ambitious for the company.

OTHER PARTNERS: Aquarians tend to get along with all signs, but can be persistent and rebellious, undemonstrative and exacting, whatever their mood.

Aquarius-Aries: Very dynamic, both want to be leader, should divide their powers.

Aquarius-Taurus: Difficult, but Taurus will help organise a system, to make money.

Aquarius-Gemini: Wonderful, and both can work at more than one thing at a time.

Aquarius-Cancer: Cancer would look after all the administration, Aquarius the ideas.

Aquarius-Leo: Excellent, they can do anything, as long as it is exciting and fun.

Aquarius-Virgo: If Virgo can take the changes, then they work painstakingly.

Aquarius-Libra: Good. Libra loves to do research, complementing the partnership.

Aquarius-Scorpio: Not easy, but Scorpio could be a wonderful inspiration.

Aquarius-Sagittarius: The more chances taken by this team, the luckier they'll be.

Aquarius-Capricorn: Difficult if not working for a common cause. Both stubborn.

Aquarius-Aquarius: Perfectly wonderful, they understand each other's idiosyncrasies.

Aquarius-Pisces: Fair. Aquarius will be too demanding, Pisces lazy at times.

PISCES AS PARTNER

BEST BETS: Pisces is attracted to working with other water signs Cancer, Scorpio and fellow Pisces. They need to feel wanted and this combination of signs is sufficiently emotional and unselfish to make the whole thing seem romantic. They will all work devotedly for each other. The Cancer Patriot, the Scorpio Magician, and the Pisces Doctor can work wonders for themselves and for others. Virgo and Capricorn are other partners to consider as they have traits that Pisces needs. Virgo is good with detail and therefore can organise the hard working Pisces into making more money and making a more efficient schedule. Capricorn has large business plans in mind, and with Pisces many dreams will come true.

EXPANSION: Only if their partner wants it. So the partner has to decide early and discuss it in detail. There will never be any fight over new ventures as Pisces will be loyal whatever the two do. The major problem comes if they are asked to make the final decision, in which case they will procrastinate, and change their minds. They want to please the other and by doing so will make personal sacrifices and moral compromises.

EVERYDAY EXPENSES: Pisces spend more than most people on medical expenses, pills, vitamins, but very little on office and business affairs. Partners can be happy that this is a fairly conservative person, but they may be too careful and frugal at times. Using recycled paper, however, is wonderful for conservation and ecology and re-using envelopes and packing by using labels are some of their good money saving ideas.

FINANCIAL CRISIS: Pisces become very emotional and can burst into tears if the crisis is their own, but they handle other's problems with efficient and systematic concern. Don't let Pisces take on too much responsibility or think that the crisis is as big as it appears. They could try to dismiss the problem altogether, escaping into a series of fantasies, lies and camouflage, rather than admitting the truth. They could also lose all confidence in themselves and give up big business and enter a convent or a monastery!

POLICY DECISIONS: By all means discuss them in great detail with Pisces, but don't expect a straight answer, or opinion. Diplomatic and afraid of hurting others they will hide behind tact, charm, and outright lies in some instances and partners will find it hard to perceive their true feelings. For this reason always question the motivation behind any changes of policy that Pisces makes, even when made for a kind and generous cause.

OTHER PARTNERS: Everyone would love to have Pisces as a partner, they are devoted and loyal, and, apart from the confusion they create, are reliable workers.

Pisces-Aries: Aries may demand more from Pisces than they are willing to give.

Pisces-Taurus: Taurus would make profitable Pisces' talents and skills.

Pisces-Gemini: Weak, as both tend to exaggerate and hide the true facts.

Pisces-Cancer: Excellent. Much success in joint ventures. A close relationship.

Pisces-Leo: Leo will make Pisces have more fun, but still not a profitable team.

Pisces-Virgo: Excellent. Hard working, devoted and will attain much success.

Pisces-Libra: Very weak in business. Good in non-profit making organisations.

Pisces-Scorpio: Very powerful business team. Scorpio pushes Pisces to the top.

Pisces-Sagittarius: Difficult. Sagittarius would lose interest in long term jobs.

Pisces-Capricorn: Very good. Materially successful. Both work for mutual results.

Pisces-Aquarius: Reasonable. If the cause is right they will both work hard for it.

Pisces-Pisces: Good, but can be confusing if one doesn't take the lead.

Chapter Seven
Long-term plans

'This very remarkable man
Commends a most practical plan;
You can do what you want
If you don't think you can't,
So don't think you can't if you can.'

Charles Inge

Planning ahead is something we all know we should do but usually manage to put off until something forces it to our attention. The earlier you start planning for your retirement, begin long-term investments and make provision for supporting your loved ones after your inevitable death, the easier and better will be your long-range strategies.

Retirement is probably the most painful subject for most of us so let's take a look at some practical notions about it.

You don't have to retire at 65. You can retire earlier or later. It's up to you to decide just when. You will, however, need to accumulate financial resources to keep you fed and warm – you can't depend on a pension for all of that – and those resources have to be earned.

Some facts about retirement:

* it ranks ninth of the top 40 stress producers,

* current predictions are that the average retirement age 20 years hence will be 52 years – meaning that a worker in his mid-30s today will, with life expectancy increasing, face a quarter of a century of retirement.

* lifestyle and mental changes brought on by retirement come when the retiree is at his least flexible both mentally and physically.

* your job performance will be affected for years before you do retire – just by the apprehension that builds up as it approaches.

Let's consider the basic steps towards making a sound retirement plan.

You will have certain problems to face on retirement. Money, health, where to live, legal responsibilities and increased free time are some of them. By planning ahead, by using your astrological traits to your own advantage and by considering the trends predicted in the last chapter of this book, you should be able to make a reasonably intelligent estimate of what's in store. Some of the points are not mystical at all – you will be able to develop a financial plan – budgeting, investments, estate planning, tax changes, pensions and so on, by reading this book and by making it your business to find out.

You should provide for adequate medical care as part of your pre-retirement package; you shouldn't neglect your psychological health (knowing your star-induced strengths and weaknesses will help); you should make obvious provision for your probably reduced financial circumstances – ensuring, for example that you have adequate housing, transportation and perhaps some lifestyle changes with your smaller income, too.

Then there are social factors to be considered – where you will live. Is it wise to retire to a new place? Leaving behind all your social life, your family, your friends simply to live in a more pleasant town might not always make good sense – discuss it with relatives and think it out carefully.

You will have more leisure time when you retire. How will you fill it? Will the transition from being an active employee to a leisured member of the unemployed undermine you? Finally, you should spend some time becoming aware of the legal pitfalls to which you might fall prey. You might consider selling your house so what are the legal pitfalls, who is there likely to cause legal difficulties over a will, for example? Are your business affairs in order? Are you likely to become a victim of a swindler of the kind who makes older people a target? Will you take an increased part in community activities or will you start a second, perhaps part-time career?

We can't do more than raise these questions, there are too many variables and each individual case has to be considered on its merits. But if you are aware of some of the pitfalls and plan ahead you can sidestep them. Let's look at the individual zodiac signs and see what patterns are best suited to their lives, and to their long-range planning.

ARIES (21st March – 19th April)

Your best way of starting a retirement plan is to plunge in headlong at once. Even if your retirement account – opened at the bank as a separate savings account – has only a few pounds in it, you will have taken that critical, concrete first step. You Ariens should concentrate on two things: on setting up a substantial emergency savings fund – which you might already have planned, after preparing your monthly budget; and also on planning now to establish some extra sources of income when you retire. You can do it by investment or by beginning a hobby that will earn money for you, so you'll have another income when you retire.

Good money-earning hobbies for you could include a mail order club, a part-time travel agency or social club with several annual outings, or something connected with gardening or farming – you might start a vegetable garden, with intentions of expanding it and selling surplus later.

Good investments for you are ones you can actually see making dramatic leaps forward from time to time. Rare coins, stamps, books or precious stones – especially coloured stones – are suitable. They have enjoyed tremendous surges in value and equally dramatic losses at times, too, but overall they have shown appreciable gains. You'll enjoy the drama of the peaks and valleys of earnings performance, safe in the knowledge that overall they are rising. Put aside a certain amount of money each month for investment.

Next: make a will. See a lawyer and get it done properly – otherwise you will subject your loved ones to possible distress. Make sure, too, that you have adequate life insurance cover.

Consider where you will live – you will be happy moving away from your present home. Check again under the best places for you to live and see if one of them couldn't be your retirement home.

If you expect to have a reduced standard of living, plan now what you will be most willing to give up. It might be entertainment – so plan ahead to provide cheaper, equally enjoyable substitutes. Instead of visiting the theatre, see if there isn't a local amateur group you can join.

TAURUS (20th April – 21st May)
Organised, moneywise Taureans like you can make your own retirement a joy, thanks to your ability to plan ahead. Concentrate on the financial aspects first. Set about creating extra sources of retirement income; check that your company pension plan will be in line with the kind of money you will need; plan your long-term investments for maximum effect.

You will be happy putting money into municipal bonds, into property and into the slightly riskier but highly-rewarding 'nostalgic collectibles' market. As an organised Taurean, you will spend your money, so the element of risk – purchases that might yield very highly or hardly at all – isn't unacceptable. Old camera equipment or Victorian mechanical toys are very much your line. However, there is an area of collectibles you should avoid: all those coins not intended for spending, the medals that will never grace a military uniform and the collectors' plates, plaques and miscellaneous objects that are made just to be collected. They historically show the worst record of appreciation. If you like them and want them to enhance your home decor, fine – but don't choose them as investments – they make less than 5% per annum, on average.

Other long-range plans: make a will and update it every few years. Don't make it a Do-It-Yourself effort with a cheap pre-printed form from the stationer's. Spend a few pounds on having a competent lawyer draw it up. You'll save your family considerable trouble and possibly great lumps of estate tax.

Calculate on how your standard of living will change with retirement and your probably-reduced income, and make plans for overcoming the difference. Make sure you have adequate medical insurance; that your plans for activities are well under way – you'll have far more leisure time and busy Taureans hate to be bored; create an emergency savings fund just for those unforeseen events that need ready cash right away. When you've carried out these measures, you'll be a contented Bull and will be able to settle into a happy and active retirement without major worries.

GEMINI (22nd May – 20th June)
Restive, creative Geminis quite like the idea of retirement from the everyday working world because, you reason, it will give you more time for the things you enjoy, travel, books and the chance to work with your hands. You'll certainly have the time, but your astrological traits mean that usually you won't have the money because you won't plan ahead.

Retiring from work means a reduction in income, as a general rule, and unless you put in some timely planning you'll not have enough income to support yourself in the manner to which you have become accustomed. Frankly, you're likely to be broke. Don't dismiss the idea just because it's 20 or more years away. Start a retirement account now with cash put aside each month, with an investment programme, with insurances or property that can provide you with an income later. A small amount put away regularly now will make all the difference later – don't just rely on your State pension or company retirement plan – they probably won't be enough, with inflation running at the rate it is.

Make a down payment on a piece of property and pay for it before you retire – if it is a house or flat, you can rent the place out – and property values won't decline. Buy long-term municipal bonds, begin a coin or paintings collection that you can realise later. Take out life insurance policies of the endowment kind – your insurance broker will advise what is best for you in your particular circumstances. Begin a modest stock portfolio, it need not cost the earth.

Long before you are thinking of retiring, make your will. Specify who will get what – and work to make the legacies you are going to leave worthwhile ones. Do it through a lawyer – don't try to do it by yourself. The advice will be worth the money.

Consider how your living standards will change and see if you can't lessen the blow. Some Geminis who enjoy their retirement hold down two, even three small part-time jobs and love the change in routine. Remember too, to stay close to your friends and family – don't let your restless spirit cause you to uproot to some far away spot just on a whim, or you'll be lonely.

CANCER (21st June – 22nd July)

Cautious Moon Children, you don't like the idea of change and retirement, but you are prepared to be convinced of the need for long-term planning to cope with it. Your best investments are in property and in your home. Many Crabs buy another, smaller, retirement home. Then, when the day comes, they know the area and the people and can make the transition painlessly enough. Remember that change for an older Crab is not easy – so prepare for it when you are better equipped mentally to deal with it.

Making money to help cope with the financial burdens of retirement isn't as big a problem for you as it can be for other zodiac signs. You usually have a proper set of insurance plans, investments (often a collection of antique silver or old weapons or brass and copper) which you could liquidate if necessary and you generally go about setting up a retirement fund, pension fund or similar alternative source of income when you are in your late 30s or early 40s.

Plan to live somewhere congenial – your heart is where your home is – and warmer places, near the sea or a lake are ideal for you. Make a will in plenty of time and remember to update it from time to time. Use a lawyer to help set up the provisions of the will and to help you with tax considerations.

Take care of practical things like ensuring you have adequate clothing, a good car and the sort of garden tools, household equipment and the like that you will need. You should have paid off your mortgage before you retire, and you'll be happy to retreat into your shell to write a little, to read a lot and to enjoy the company of your family and friends more. And there's another consideration: don't move too far away from family. You'll have more leisure, at first anyway, and will enjoy associating more with your grandchildren – so don't be too far away from them.

Last but not least, see what community activities you can become involved with, in your area. You enjoy social contact and being busy – so keep that way and enjoy a long and happy retirement. Just plan it now.

LEO (23rd July – 22nd August)
Retirement might sound like a bad word to you Leos, but it can be a chance for you to fulfill some of your lifelong ambitions because at last you'll have the time to sit down and begin doing them. But first you have to make financial provision for the lazy, hazy days of retirement, for the purchase of that splendid home you've always meant to buy

but never could. The only way for you is through solid, long-term investments.

You might well put some small monies into stocks and bonds, you might open a building society account against the day you are 65, but your heart will rarely be in seeing just a line of black figures in a savings book or statement. Instead, invest in something that will appeal to your lordly instincts – in gold. You can buy individual Krugerrands, or Mexican 50-peso pieces, or British sovereigns or even small gold bars. You can even buy into the South African or Canadian gold mining company shares and gloat secretly over the 15% per annum yield (but don't buy through telephone salesmen). However you buy, gold is the key to your heart and later financial security. Take it.

Plan carefully just what you will do with your retirement, avoiding over-enthusiastic rushing into every project you hear about. Will you change your style of living? Take out proper insurance coverage, especially to protect your loved ones in case of your own untimely exit from life's stage; make a comprehensive will with the aid of a competent lawyer; and create an emergency savings fund for the day the chimney of your splendid baronial home falls off. You have a practical side – let it have full rein and make some careful provision for the future. After all, what might happen 20 years hence will be important to you then and a little forward planning now could cushion the painful blows you might receive.

VIRGO (23rd August – 22nd September)
Yours is one of the most prudent signs of the Zodiac, and you invariably live up to your astrological traits. Here's one of the best pieces of advice you'll ever get: plan ahead for your retirement.

You should concentrate on establishing a proper pension plan – don't assume if you are employed that the one your employer has is the best for you – and make regular donations to it (they are tax exempt). Take out proper insurance policies, for health, in case of a deterioration later and as endowments, to assure you of income when you need it. Begin an emergency savings fund – for emergencies, not a special dress or a splendid holiday; plan extra sources of income such as selling craftwork or taking on a part-time job when you are retired. Make sure that your financial affairs are in some sort of order – you should have paid off your house mortgage before you retire, you shouldn't have any major debts and you should be aware of any tax considerations – perhaps a pleasant refund, thanks to your likely reduction of income.

Try to plan for the bite inflation will take from your fixed income, and see if there isn't a way to guard against it. Consider investments in areas which suit your star sign, so you will continue to put money into those accounts during your working life. Some excellent areas suited to you are antiques (although you are often reluctant to part with them), books, oriental rugs – a spectacular, if slightly risky area which has been appreciating at around 15% per annum in the early 1980s; and precious stones. The better buys of late have been coloured stones like emeralds, sapphires and topazes instead of the more traditional diamonds.

Make a will – with legal help. That's important if you want your heirs to receive things the way you wish, and perhaps even to lessen the tax bite on them. Plan where you want to live, what you want to do with your new leisure, and be cautious of the swindlers who prey on older people with phony sales or service offers.

In other words, be the wise, pennywise Virgin your sign says you are.

LIBRA (23rd September – 22nd October)
You'll work a lifetime to earn your retirement and you might well not get all the financial rewards you deserve, hard-working Libran. You see, yours is a sign of service to others,

and you invariably put yourself second. You think nothing of diligent service, self-sacrifice for others (especially your children) and making financial hardships a part of your everyday life, so long as someone benefits. But you seldom make your own self the beneficiary. Your best plan for long-term financial success is to consider your own interests, if not first – we can't change the way you are made – but at least second.

You know that one day you'll be out of harness, out to pasture – all the best clichés for ending work – so plan for it. It isn't immoral to have leisure time to do just what you want. Start today taking some practical steps to set up a retirement account. Open a savings bank account, or a deposit account. Visit your local building society or speak to a stockbroker. With a small monthly sum put aside, you can assure the future. Invest in property – it suits your personality to have a solid, bricks and mortar investment. A mixed portfolio of investments can be built up gradually, and they can work for you. Some stocks and bonds (especially in anything to do with music, orchestras or music companies), antiques or silver, a little gold – preferably gold mining company shares – and a few riskier but high-yielding speculations like brass and copper, farm implements, old weapons or old toys will add interest as you build your portfolio.

Also, because you epitomise the work ethic (try going to a fancy dress party as that, some time!) you'll be happy planning a second career or at least part-time job when you do retire. Consider things lika a plant or flower shop, interior decorating advice, any kind of craft work, metal working or silversmithing. If you start your second career as a hobby 10 or 20 years before you need it as an income source, you might easily be surprised at the excellence of the results.

Lastly – do make a competent will, with legal advice. Update it regularly, as you should also update insurance on your home, life and car, and plan for a happy retirement – you'll have earned it.

SCORPIO (23rd October – 21st November).
Assuming that you'll somehow manage, somehow get by when the time comes to retire just won't do, Scorpions. Most people naturally shrink from the idea of growing old, and positively wilt away from the harsh question of how they'll manage financially after they stop working – but you are among the more extreme cases. You try to ignore it altogether. Is it so hard to face? Once you have convinced yourself that you should take action early, matters will be so much easier for you because you can put all your fine Scorpion attributes of tenacity, regeneration and determination together to help establish an income for your later years.

The best plan for you is to establish a good pension plan, one where a fixed amount is deducted from your income each week or month before you get to it. But you must sit down and calculate how inflation is likely to affect the plan – what seems like an adequate sum today will look sorry indeed after 20 years' worth of inflation. Try to make your pension plan one that will rise with inflation – if it doesn't, you'll have to boost your pre-retirement income. Set aside something during the last 10 years at least of your working life, aiming to invest in mutual funds, growth stocks or high-grade bonds. Consider using some of your current income to buy an annuity, or a life insurance policy or income-producing property so you'll be pegged in the inflation market and your income won't be fixed (and therefore depreciate). Then, of course, you'll have to plan on withdrawing a portion of your capital reserves each year of your retirement – this calculation will give you a clue to how much you'll need to accumulate based on your life expectancy, the amount of other pensions or fixed incomes and your life style.

Apart from your regular stocks, real estate, savings and building society income, you might want to invest in some more glamorous and high-yielding areas. Consider coins, stamps, rare books, paintings or prints and antiques. These are all investments which – properly chosen – have been running in the 10–15% per annum yield and which promise to maintain those levels. Avoid the made-to-order collectibles, the memorial plaques and medals of silver or porcelain which show very much slower appreciation.

An interesting if highly speculative area is children's comic books. Some examples which could be purchased for a few pence in 1939 are currently valued at over £8,000!

SAGITTARIUS (22nd November – 21st December)

You Sagittarians are among the most confident signs of the zodiac, and things like long-range planning really don't interest you except as an exercise for someone else. Please consider yourselves, and make contingency plans. You *should* have a will, long-term investments, insurances and a retirement plan. It's all very well not wanting to consider the possibilities, or assuming that you'll muddle through somehow but you can make your own later life so much more comfortable, with a little planning, that you should sit down now and start using your creative mind to create a financial future.

First, make a will. It will allow you to take an inventory of what you have and where it should go. Do make it with a lawyer's advice as he could save you a lot of hard cash, especially when it comes to estate planning.

Decide when you want to retire – it need not be at 65, but could be earlier or later. Then you can start calculating how much money you'll need to live on and how you are going to get it. Sagittarians like you generally prefer to begin a second career after you retire from your first one. You are attracted to sport and sporting events, to entertainment centres like discotheques, cinemas and resorts. You might wish to open a small mountain lodge, a restaurant or a caravan site – these are all excellent Sagittarian occupations ideally suited to your temperament. Start making investments now in buying property you can develop later; put money into mutual funds and life insurance policies that will yield an income in the future.

Your best investments can include putting money into businesses like landscape gardening or tree services; apparel shops; gift shops and guard services; moving and storage companies; lumber yards or carpentry shops or services, and taxi services.

Some investments in gold – whether coins or mining company shares or other metals, zinc, steel, copper, etc. – will be good for you, as will a small collection of some kind – be it of unusual chessmen, defunct stock certificates, old maps (an increasingly popular and expensive hobby) or old prints. Photographs from the last century are becoming increasingly valuable, and this is a chance for your discerning and artistic eye to make money for you – selecting photos with merit and growth potential. All you have to do is make that start, Sagittarians – your abilities will do the rest.

CAPRICORN (22nd December – 19th January)
Plan your retirement Capricorns, the way you plan those sales or military campaigns when you're day dreaming – with dash, flair and precision. You are about the best-suited of the zodiac to plan ahead, because you have qualities of organisation, determination and tenacity of purpose ideally suited for the purpose.

Your steps are simple enough: decide when you will retire, how much you will need to live on, then what will be your income. The difference is what you have to begin now to build up. You might consider a paying hobby that can become more important when you retire; income from property you purchase now; income from stocks and bonds (although there is an element of risk in the stocks, of course) plus a savings account, an emergency cash reserve and perhaps a collection of increasingly-valuable items you can sell later when you need to realise the equity you have built up in them.

You will take sensible and commonsense steps like paying off the mortgage on your home before you retire, of course, plus making sure that your clothes, car, household furnishings and so on are in good condition. In other words, you will try to prepare yourself financially for a time of reduced income.

What you must take into account, however, is the increased leisure time you'll have available. You must not overlook a plan to keep yourself actively occupied after you stop full-time work. Involve yourself in community affairs – you make the kind of organiser most groups love. Raise funds for your church, social group or local library. Start a vegetable garden or a mail-order catalogue sales outlet. Many Capricorns, with your affinity for the military, will collect military memorabilia, or accumulate facts for a regimental history, or organise old comrades' reunions. You'll sell poppies for Remembrance Day, raise funds for the local British Legion club, for the Sea Cadets or other semi-military group. And you're good at it – so use your talents.

Areas to consider: take out life insurance policies that will mature when you retire; make a proper will, with legal help; don't move too far from your family when you do retire; do make provision for your possibly poorer health as you age (for example see that a new home is easy to run, with a smaller garden, fewer difficult stairs and so forth). Then, Capricorns, settle back to enjoy the fruits of your work.

AQUARIUS (20th – 19th January)
You Aquarians aren't mercenary or materialistic, you're humanitarians, not hostages to money, but you must be prepared to make some fiscal plan for your later years. Think of it as a sacrifice you are making to ensure the comfort and security of your loved ones and you'll do it more easily.

There are some basics you'll need to do: make a proper will, and update it from time to time. Do use a lawyer to help draft it. Decide how much money you will need to live comfortably, then decide how best to raise that money. Your retirement fund should include an emergency savings fund and you should expect it to be boosted by some extra sources of earned income – you Aquarians are too active, too progressive just to sit back and live off your capital.

Among the easiest ways for you to save are by taking out long-term insurance policies that will mature when you retire, or soon after; buying real estate for income property (a small deposit now, payments for 10 or 20 years and it's yours as you retire); putting savings in a building society savings account, some municipal bonds and a mixed portfolio of stocks and shares. You will enjoy investing in the electronics industry – there are some hot properties, some sleepers and some duds, so it's a chancy but interesting field – and in anything connected with travel, foreign languages, teaching and art. Consider starting a collection of postage stamps of investment quality; or of collecting rare books, old farm implements or old weaponry. They are interesting areas for you and although they shouldn't be the basis of your retirement fund, can form a substantial part of it – if you are prepared to realise some of your assets later.

Look out for the frankly adventurous investments like sea-farming schemes or even a share in a racehorse. You have strong intuition and won't lose money and although the schemes might not make as much as other ideas, you'll have fun backing them.

Remember to take precautions about safeguarding your health – proper insurance is a must – and consider now where you would like to live when you do retire. Try taking some holidays there, perhaps even purchasing your retirement home now, as an investment.

PISCES (20th February – 20th March)
The inspiration you Pisceans need to help you make long-

term plans is to think of them as security. If you know that whatever comes, you'll be financially independent, and through your own actions and resources, you'll have a special glow in your lives that will make all the sacrifices worthwhile. You have a strong sense of destiny, and you believe that whatever you do will one day come back to you. It makes long-term efforts worthwhile, because you know that anything given up now will be amply rewarded later. That's not only a soothing thought, it's a sound economic principle.

Your best retirement plan will concentrate on setting up secure sources of income. For you, with your talents, we suggest starting a second career now, one that you can do part-time today and which you can expand into a lucrative occupation when you finally do retire. You'll be attracted to graphics, calligraphy or artwork; to home decorating; to consultancies of various kinds – from income tax to landscape gardening and to ventures like riding academies, nursery schools, plumbing, gift shops, hairdressing and dog-breeding.

Plan where you will live when you retire, too. Most Pisceans love to be near the seashore, or by a lake or river. Consider buying a retirement home in your ideal spot – then using it as a holiday home or as a rental property until it is time for you to move in. By living in what will be your new home, you'll get to know its advantages and disadvantages, to lessen the shock of a move to a strange place and you'll have the appreciation in value of it or of your existing home as working capital.

Take out life insurance policies, a wide spread of stocks and bonds, check that the pension plan in which you are enrolled is a viable one with realistic rewards; establish an emergency savings fund; set aside regular amounts each month in municipal bonds or a building society and even start an antiques or other valuables collection you can later sell, at an appreciable increase in value.

Make a comprehensive will, with legal help; ensure that your medical care will be adequate, or take out insurance to see that it is; pay off your home mortgage before you retire and ensure that major purchase items lika a car, furnishings or appliances are all in good contition for your retirement while you are still working. Then settle back to enjoy yourself. Good luck.

Chapter Eight
Tight corners

*'"I am the lone lorn creetur" were Mrs Gummidge's words ...
"and everythink goes contrairy with me."'*

Charles Dickens

Don't we all know that dreadful feeling of everything going 'contrairy' with us, too? It's normal and natural that at times our best-laid schemes go astray, that even the finest financial planning won't cope with the exploded furnace, the cracked damp-course or the lifeless car engine.

Sometimes the disasters are worse – a medical condition that can put the poor unfortunate out of work; redundancy, with its similar effects, and the host of other disasters which can turn a once confident wage-earner into a demoralised welfare recipient.

Curiously enough, those times are hardest not for the financial pinch, but for the undermining of an individual's sense of worth. It can be hard to walk into the unemployment bureau, to find oneself not just unemployed but evidently unemployable, this week at least. It is especially hard for the recently laid-off older worker, who realistically assesses his chances as worse than those of his younger colleagues.

At those times, he'll need not just financial aid, but a boost to morale as well. This chapter is aimed at helping you understand what is likely to lead you into financial difficulties, how your astrological strengths will help you cope, what practical steps you can take and how you should handle creditors and complaints.

You can obtain a peep at the trends which will be forthcoming in your life, in the last chapter. You can see how using your own traits to shape the best budget for you can help avoid the practical pitfalls if you refer back to chapter two. This chapter is a lifebelt, thrown to the debtor sinking in a financial bog, aimed at helping him survive immediately, then at finding a long-term way out of the mess by making a few simple habit changes.

Most people gradually work themselves into financial problems by simply not budgeting at all. They live from hand to mouth, justifying it by the not-always-untrue statement: 'There isn't enough to go around – we can't afford to budget.' Yet, if the truth were known and a budget made, most people would be astonished to see just what they *do* spend money on – and that's the start of a savings campaign. We'll spell out your weaknesses – astrologically, that is – and inclinations in money-spending in a short while, sign by sign. First, there is one area that is common to all the zodiac: how to handle complaints.

Often complaints, about work, the product you make, your children, pets, domestic habits or debts can lead to considerable financial outlay. Consider if you will the steps generally involved in handling a complaint against you. Usually it will involve something you've done (or haven't done) either in the product you make, or sell; or in your everyday work. It might be that a neighbour is complaining about your family pets, your children, the noise you or they make or some other nuisance – in his terms – that is bothering him. The first rule is to remember that a soft answer turns away wrath. Hold your tongue and your temper, and find out exactly what the complaint is. This is the commonest mistake – people assume they know, start arguing and watch the whole thing escalate. A little patience now could save a potential court appearance later – with its attendant financial burdens. Be sympathetic and reasonably co-operative – although you should make no hasty commitments at this stage. Simply ascertain what is the problem. Be prepared to take your time over making a decision if there is a reasonable element of doubt. Tell the complainant you'll investigate the matter, and consider it carefully. Take his name, telephone number and any other information that is appropriate to the complaint and make a tactical withdrawal. Don't sweep your skirts up around you and swoosh out. After an hour or two away from the source of your new problem, you will be better able to assess the complaint and act on it. No hasty action, no immediate redress or vow you'll never give redress – just a timely cooling-off period for you both. Then make your counter-offer. You know it is reasonable – and so will the complainant because he too has had time to recover from the (for most people) nerve-wracking effort of complaining. If it is a serious matter, consult a friend, the Citizens' Advice Bureau or a lawyer.

Use similar, low-key approaches when you too are making a complaint but let the person you are complaining to know that you expect a significant reply. Offer him an option: 'This was wrong – will you replace it? If not, will you refund my money?' Remember, most people feel they aren't really to blame for a mistake, or in the case of a trader, for faulty goods they have merely passed on to you. It isn't entirely reasonable to dash in screaming – go in with a constructive attitude and seek a replacement, or a refund. If it isn't forthcoming, the local Chamber of Commerce or Better Business Bureau or even the trader's own association can often be helpful. But first try a direct, courteous approach. It works almost all the time.

Let's now take a look at the jinxes and Jonahs in your astrological make-up – what factors most commonly cause you to come unglued financially?

ARIES (21st March – 19th April)
The tight financial corners you'll most often find yourself in are because you've over-reached yourself, thanks to your tremendous sense of self-confidence. You probably saw the

warning signs, but ignored them thinking they were something you could easily take care of.

Usually your overspending has to do with entertainment, with cars or car accessories, clubs and associations or hire-purchase debts. Once in a while, sheer bad luck with a medical condition or unemployment will lay you low, too.

When you're down financially, don't consolidate your outstanding credit debts, your hire-purchase or credit card or instalment debts into one monthly payment, however attractive and pseudo-logical it sounds. You'll end up paying more, not less.

Unless you have already fled the country, notify your creditors that, for the following reasons, you are temporarily unable to meet your debts. Offer to pay off at least the interest on your outstanding loans – you'll find most creditors surprisingly helpful. After all, it is in their interests too that you pay off what you owe.

Use your nimble Aries brain to review your budget – or even to make one (see chapter two) and keep your Aries confidence boosted that you'll soon be out of the woods. Usually, a month or two of belt-tightening and a close look at exactly what you are spending your money on will sort out the problem.

Last but not least – once you have started back with a clean sheet, follow the proper principles of budgeting to ensure that you don't slip back into your old ways – and back too into debts you can't handle.

TAURUS (20th April – 21st May)
For you, the slippery downward path to financial embarrassment is usually because of your taste for hedonism. You enjoy the good things in life far too much for your own financial good. You tend to overspend on food and drink, on entertaining your friends and on entertaining yourself.

You're likely to be extravagant on holiday spending and on

credit care debts. You are too easily tempted and it leads you into financial difficulties that aren't worth the original pleasure.

Most Taureans like you are organised enough not to get into deep financial jeopardy – but if you do, take some advice from your accountant or legal expert. Review your budget, too, to see where it is all going – and see if you can't put your spending on a diet.

Don't, however, underspend – even when you are trying to save – on certain things. Your health is important. Don't put it at any kind of risk. That might involve some modest spending on preventive medicine, ensuring, for example that you get regular exercise, perhaps even an inexpensive weekend away to rest and relax.

Your methodical nature also ensures that you will be comfortable taking proper steps to clear your debts – perhaps in smaller amounts than you would wish, but with regular payments nonetheless. Make sure that you inform your creditors of your new circumstances.

GEMINI (22nd May – 20th June)
All that glitters might not be gold – but it often costs enough to get it and you can't always pay for it. Geminis like you are prone to overspend recklessly on the glittering rewards – the splendid car, ostentatious clothes or dazzling jewellery – heedless of how you're ever practically going to pay for them.

You'll often plunge on buying new appliances for the home when the old ones were perfectly good for another year or two or you'll lavish on a splendid meal for half a dozen of your friends on a whim. Just try to live up to your new image as a responsible, budget-conscious Twin. Think of yourself as two people – a sober, industrious banker and a gay, sparkling Twin-about-Town. Then let the sparkling Twin sparkle as much as he wants – within the budget.

If you do get into fiscal fixes, get some advice from a

qualified friend; pin-point the source of your troubles and then set about drawing in your horns to put the figures in your bank statement back into the black. One very good way that you Geminis like, is to take a part-time job of a temporary nature – perhaps selling sports events programmes, or doing a little moonlighting from your regular occupation. Do it just as a temporary measure though, otherwise, if you think it's for five years or more, you'll soon lose interest. Set yourself a goal of so many hundreds of pounds, reach it and then quit. But don't lapse into your old spendthrift ways – remember the other side of your personality – the sober, budget-conscious banker, and please him, too.

CANCER (21st June – 22nd July)

Your chief cause of trouble is that you poke your heads in the sand and hope the problem will go away. You'll recognise that certain actions will probably cause you fiscal grief later, but you'll hope that they won't. Then you'll be gloomily satisfied to see you were right after all.

Your weaknesses are food and household things. You'll overspend on having a larder full of good things – just in case friends drop by and so you can practically choke them with a display of your culinary prowess. You'll also overspend on having every single new kitchen gadget you can find, on buying new furnishings for your home, on hire-purchase of furniture and appliances like fridges, washers, dryers and televisions. Then you'll be shocked to find you have hardly any money to pay for them.

Take the commonsense steps: find out where the money really is going, and it might be hard for you to be honest with yourself because you'll discount those boxes of chocolates as 'only occasional spendings' but they aren't. Next, notify your creditors and request that they give you a little more time to pay – or allow you to pay off only the interest on your debts until you get financially straight again.

Finally – start visiting your friends at their homes for a change – you'll save a fortune!

LEO (23rd July – 22nd August)
The most probable financial quicksands for you Leos are those concerned with clothing, shoes, personal grooming and personal accoutrements. You're most likely to overspend on something dazzling to wear than you are to lose everything gambling.

When you Leos over-reach, you do it dramatically – you never make some quiet, anonymous slide into poverty – you go out in a champagne-and-caviar splash. You'll plunge into bankruptcy with the same abandon as you enjoy a party – with all of your enjoy-life-to-the-full tastebuds bursting to discover this new flavour – poverty. You play hard, and work hard. The trouble is, you do have a tendency to play a little more expensively than your income will justifiy.

When it comes time to check the budget, see that you haven't too many expensive club memberships on it, that your clothes bill is reasonable by the standards of others, not just your own. You'll probably be astonished to find out how little (in your eyes) others spend on clothes.

Another potential disaster area for you is at work. You are outgoing and a leader, but often your superiors in the workplace don't want that all the time. Be careful not to give the impression of arrogance or vanity – you really aren't, but it can strike people that way.

Should you get into financial trouble, don't consolidate your loans into one big one; don't take out personal loans from the bank to give 'temporary' relief that will only make matters worse and don't gamble.

VIRGO (23rd August – 22nd September)
Loyal, careful Virgos just like you are only likely to stumble into a fiscal mess in a few ways. You'll most often find yourself

struggling because you gave too much of your own time, money and efforts to helping others. You'll also sometimes find yourself in trouble because you had your mind on other, more important things than money – and never monitored the outgoings properly. Sometimes you'll find yourself in the red after a medical or domestic crisis. Only rarely, however, will you have some fault of your own to truly blame for financial disaster.

If you are finding those ominous letters OD after your bank balance, don't immediately cut back on any areas which could affect your health. Don't stint on a proper diet, or on medical care or proper clothing.

Do notify your creditors, and ask them if you can have more time to pay, or at least pay off just the interest for the time being. Do review your budget, and do cut back on the use of credit cards, too – using them to delay payments won't really help matters. You should be using your analytical mind to see ways to change your patterns of spending – on a permanent basis.

LIBRA (23rd September – 22nd October)
The times you Librans find yourselves in a pickle over money are the times you leave money matters to someone else to manage. There's your problem – and there's your answer. You have a superb capacity for partnership, but you do tend rather to abdicate responsibilities in financial matters when frankly, you'd do a better job.

You might overspend a little – rarely enough to make major inroads, though – on plants and plantholders, on antiques, silver, brass, copper, musical instruments or music lessons, language lessons, tapes, records – anything that is, well, frankly 'improving'. It sounds like the curriculum for a Swiss finishing school – and that's what you secretly like to spend money on.

Where the trouble comes is that you make one

commitment, take on another, spend on a third, fourth and
fifth and suddenly relatively insignificant debts have become
a snowballing monster. Your answer: stop making except-
ions for 'this particular case'.

When you do find you're in this situation, take a long hard,
hurtful look at your outgoings – and set a determined budget
for those plants, macramé, antiques, silver, etc.

SCORPIO (23rd October – 21st November)
Major financial problems for you Scorpios will mostly come
when you overspend on credit cards, on hire-purchase or
other deferred payment schemes, on drink or on gambling.
You handle money reasonably well as a general rule – but
sometimes you'll throw caution to the winds, you'll risk
money in shady speculations, you'll live riotously, with little
thought for tomorrow – until it comes..

Don't be tempted to try to recoup your losses with another
speculation. Don't ignore your debts – do notify creditors, do
make small payments on your debts (often an obliging
creditor who only wants his money back, after all, will agree
to take just the interest on the outstanding money).

Don't be flippant, arrogant or abusive about being broke –
it's not what your creditors want to hear. Review your budget,
cut back on obvious overspending (you are astute enough to
know what's overspent, Scorpions, unlike many in the
zodiac) and try to cut back on the sometimes excessive use
you make of your credit cards.

SAGITTARIUS (22nd November – 21st December)
Sports and sporting equipment are the commonest downfall
of you astrological Archers. You are far too often
overstocked on expensive, faddish and fashionable equipment. You simply must have new ski poles with bends in them
– although you only ski twice a year. You simply must have an

expensive racing bicycle – although you always use your car and it costs your budget dearly.

You'll spend on entertaining friends, on new household appliances every couple of years, on splendid holidays. You'll also spend on an intangible that won't show on your budget balance sheet: you'll give lots of your time and effort to community or church affairs – time you can ill-afford sometimes. You could use that time to help straighten out your own finances – why don't you?

When you have to make budget cuts, avoid making them in areas which involve education. Also avoid getting concerned with pyramid money schemes, or chain letter money-making schemes, too. Stay away from personal loans which you intend to use to bail yourself out of current debts – and don't gamble.

CAPRICORN (22nd December – 19th January)

No nonsense, Capricorns, you're too businesslike for that. You trouble is your ego, your over-abundance of self-confidence. You won't delegate, you won't accept that you aren't the Emperor Nero.

You are likely to stumble into a financial quagmire because you insist on trying to build an empire and sometimes your rigid thinking and lack of response to the suggestions of others will mean you'll diligently build on sand.

You tend to overspend on property, on having employees – but not the kind on whom you will devolve responsibility. You'll overspend on gadgetry, on pets, on protégés.

Some Capricorns can't easily handle credit and credit cards. That's another potential source of grief. A few of you insist on dining very well indeed – at great cost. It isn't necessary and it's more of a luxury than you really can afford – but as you are busy playing the imperial role, you refuse to scrimp.

Just accept that no everyone, not every Capricorn, truly is the emperor. Admit that you have talents other than the accumulation of money and power and you'll be a more mellow fellow.

AQUARIUS (20th January – 19th February)
The owners of electonics stores, from television shops to shortwave radio equipment supply depots, must cheer when they see you Aquarians. You're a sucker for the electronic gadget. You want to spend on microwave ovens, on remote control garage door-openers, on electric carrot juicers – and you do. It doesn't matter that you haven't two carrots to rub together – you'll still buy it.

You'll also spend on travel, on holidays in remote and exotic places – but when you get there all you want to do is go home and tell your friends about it. For you, travel is the thing. You're restless and careless of money when the bug comes over you.

You'll splash out on a new car far more often than you need – and then you'll lavish accessories and trimmings, tune-ups and alignments, waxes and customising on it as if there were no bottom to your pocket.

Travel less – read more. Use library books, an airline flight schedule, guide-books, a travel agent's free literature – and you'll get almost the same thrill from using your vivid imagination as you do from actually sitting in an airplane seat. Make a hobby out of shopping and planning for a holiday. Do the same when you feel the urge to buy gadgetry – shop around. And use that same rule when you itch for a new car – visit the showrooms, sit in the back seats; take test drives – and stay with your existing car. It's all the same to an imaginative Aquarian. And it's cheaper.

PISCES (20th February – 20th March)
Keeping young is your secret vice, Pisceans. You'll spend and spend on lotions and creams, on youthful clothes and a sports

car. You'll keep a lover hidden away, and entertain her or him extravagantly. Pisceans with teenage children feel it even worse, trying desperately to keep up with their offspring.

You'll suffer through sports events, have unsuitable hairstyles, wear brightly-coloured clothing and exercise desperately – just to be a Peter Pan. Well, it will all end the same way – it will either 'peter' out or it will 'pan' out. And you'll be no better off.

The fact is – you'll be poorer financially, mentally wrecked – so resist it.

Younger Pisceans will do a similar thing – they'll try to look older. It's a basic fault of you all – you are spending just to indulge your egos. You don't need to – people love you anyway, once you let down your guard.

There are some cures: marry a mature person; give more freedom to your loved ones and let them help you make major lifestyle and financial decisions or, simplest of all, accept yourself as you are. You aren't all bad. Really.

When you are in financial straits because of your habits – the answers are reasonably simple. Tell your creditors; make small payments to everybody; ask if you can make only interest payments for the time being; review your budget – and cut out all that fountain-of-youth hopeful spending. You might look a little older, but you'll feel a lot younger.

Chapter Nine
Love and money

*'Make love to every woman you meet; if you get five per cent
on your outlays it's a good investment.'*

Arnold Bennett.

It is interesting to note from the outset that it is the female
planet Venus, the Goddess of Beauty, that astrologically rules
both love and money. It could be for that simple reason that
men have traditionally lavished gifts of flowers, jewelry, furs,
cars and other expensive trappings on the woman they love.
Still it mustn't be ignored that many rich and attractive
women have also enjoyed the pleasure of spending money on
their man, not necessarily because the man was a gigolo, or
poor, but because she loved him.

It seems that the more generous and outgoing people are in
love, the more they spend on the accoutrements. If they are
mean with their romantic favours then they are likely to have
a tight wallet or purse. Yet at times, and on certain occasions, a
person may act totally out of character. Still there does
appear a definite behaviour pattern based on the sign of the
zodiac the lover is born under.

As in the chapter on business partners, each sign also reacts
differently with the other signs in love. Some combinations
are passive, others passionate, others will spend money
extravagantly, others will save money frugally. To see how
each partnership behaves financially, refer to the 'Other
Partners' listings in Chapter 6.

ARIES (21st March – 19th April)
Aries just love to spend money on their loved one – as soon as

they see something 'special' they have to buy it, and usually suffer the consequences afterwards. This impulsiveness carries on through all their various activities and enterprises. Being expansive in love, they are overly generous, wanting the biggest and the best, yet somehow they are able to finance these financial dealings through initiative and business acumen.

In order to please their loved ones they will use all their resources, working overtime, taking on extra part-time work, and even taking risks by investing in quick turn-over businesses, or gambling at the racetrack. They have been known to pawn their jewellery, cameras and other valuable possessions to make sure that their loved one(s) would not be without.

During courtship, they spend a fortune, but have great fun doing it. They feel if they have made the money once, they will certainly be able to make it again in the future. They only think of the immediate present.

Unlike the other fire signs (Leo and Sagittarius) they can also come up with gifts that do not necessarily cost very much money but are nonetheless imaginative and exciting. They are likely to present their lover with a toy Rolls-Royce, adding that they will receive the real thing in the not-too-distant-future. They like to give gifts of cars, motor bikes, motor boats, roller skates, computers and exotic gadgets.

Weddings don't have to be fancy. They may prefer to spend the money on the honeymoon, or a new business project the happy pair are about to embark on. But should they decide that a wedding is what they want, then it's all stops out, and everyone has to be invited, including the local football team, and a big brass band!

They will buy a home that is practical and near transportation even if they have a car. Freedom of movement is vital to Aries. Many Aries also work from home, or live over their business establishment. They like the idea of saving the time that others use travelling to and from work every day.

Their furniture is usually dramatic, rugged and utilitarian.

They don't go in for dainty antiques, even though many enjoy them. And they love outdoor type decor, pictures of mountains hang on their walls, as do skis, guns and sporting equipment. In clothing as well they tend towards the more rugged, sporty type, even though they love to dress up in formal wear on special occasions.

While they love children, especially the neighbour's, and their neices and nephews, they dislike the restrictions and limitations that children place on them. Usually they remain childless, unless their partner desires an offspring, then they will happily agree. Still they will spend very little on the usual extravagances of parenthood, clothes, toys and schooling. They will impose a rather rugged, spartan, self-protective regimen right from birth, and will encourage the child to start earning money as soon as possible (odd jobs, delivering newspapers, gardening, painting and other chores easily managed by nine year olds!).

There are many tax benefits in love and marriage for Aries, first they usually have their place of work and living premises as deductible items, saving money by getting the spouse to work with them (and the kids). Most holiday trips will be for 'business', searching out new prospects, and new business partners, in far away exotic places. Cars, gadgets and telephone calls all used by the wife, husband or sweetheart are most likely tax deductible. And if it will help their tax situation they are brazenly open to suggesting divorce 'for a short while'!

Should a real divorce take place, the question of how to split property and possessions has to be faced. It will be simple. Aries are not greedy or unfair. They are more willing to let their partner keep the whole lot, rather than get caught up in any emotional battles. They want their 'former' spouse to remain happy, and if they have children, that they shouldn't be in need of anything. Yet should the partner be spiteful and revengeful for some unreasonable motive, then Aries will fight – to the bitter end. And what a battle!

TAURUS (20th April – 21st May)

Taurus are known for their thrifty, materialistic nature, yet they are extremely generous in love. They are, after all, ruled by the planet Venus, and love as well as money is a vital motivating fact of their whole existence. They want a lot of both and will be willing to invest a lot of time and money in getting the 'best value'. Being exceptionally industrious and conservative they usually have a well-paying job in a conventional type of profession where their credit and annual income make it possible to buy, build and invest in anything they want.

If they want to buy something special for their loved one, they simply write a cheque, or present one of their many credit cards. But it must always be good quality, designer signed and a work of art in itself. Every gift from Taurus is an investment.

During the first weeks of courtship Taurus may appear rather tight. This is due to the fact that they hate to spend money on something that seems temporary. Once they know that the relationship is for keeps then out comes the money. Presents for the future home, the lifetime to be spent together, jewelry and accessories that will make the pair stand out at formal parties, objets d'art for the art collection, and antiques for the office or living room.

The wedding will be extravagant – the limousines, the ushers in white ties and the bridesmaids in couturier dresses. No expense will be spared for this is a once in a lifetime occasion. Taurus tends to remain loyal and usually only marries once. Also they would worry about the money affairs should they have to separate or divorce, and lose some of their 'wealth'.

Most likely they will invest in a home immediately, and furnish it with the best furniture that is available, bought on credit of course. This will be a happy home, a welcoming home, a showplace home. The furnishings while being conservative will nevertheless be expensive, and the Taurus will have great fun telling you how much everything cost, and the authenticity of the original art work. Musical instruments maybe a baby grand piano, dominate the room, and the sound system for the stereo is most likely the best and the loudest.

Children are important to Taurus so as soon as the wedding gifts are unpacked or exchanged, a family will be planned. They will spend money extravagantly on the new born babe, and spoil the child all through childhood and on through teenage life. They just want the best for the family. This gives Taurus extra motivation to earn more money, in order to support their ever growing responsibilities.

Even though Taureans try hard to keep the family together, at times they can't and divorce is the only answer. Meticulous in detail, they will itemise everything in the home and assess its value. Only then when the total value is totted up will they be willing to a clear 50-50 split. Should there be any legal battles they they will fight stubbornly for it all, resenting parting with even a penny. They become bullish!

GEMINI (22nd May – 20th June)

Gemini are extremely generous, especially with their loved ones, they are always on the look-out for a new exciting gift – a gimmicky mug, a box, a fun plaque for the wall, a book for their sweetheart. Their literary tastes range from consumer magazines (they subscribe frequently) to technical text books (their reference library is the best) to Gothic novels (the bedside bookcase is full of them) and so they expect their lover to have the same insatiable appetite … for the printed word, of course.

While their spending habits on their lovers are not extreme, and therefore not too demanding on the pocket book, they do need another job or another source of income to supplement their wages. When they start dating they are always late, so they spend a lot of extra money taking taxis rather than public transportation. But they save a lot by suggesting a night at the local library's free lecture, or visting galleries, museums and other exhibitions. They love to talk and meet other people, so public events appeal to them and their budget.

The formalities of marriage don't worry them much, and they would rather save the money for something 'more important'. If they do decide to have a wedding, then it will be simple, with friends drinking and chatting around the fire, or making new acquaintances in the line-up for food from the buffet. As Geminis tend towards more than one marriage it can get very expensive having a big banquet each time, so something simple is more suitable. A quick wedding with a Registrar will do.

They love to have children around them, but don't have the patience to be real parents, and therefore may spend money on babysitters and nannies. Yet they will buy expensive stimulating educational toys for them and of course lots of books, crayons and papers. Education is foremost in Geminis mind, and very little money gets put towards sports and other hobbies, unless it's scrabble!

As they are good candidates for the divorce courts, this will be one big major financial crisis to face early. The Gemini man may sell everything so that there will be nothing much left to share. The Gemini woman will be tempted to start hoarding and hiding items of value. In most instances the books are the only personal property that Gemini really wants, plus a fair settlement of everything else. As there are often two homes involved, then it is simple to split them and work out a fair monetary balance to be paid to the one with the smaller property. Where bank accounts are concerned, it may be wiser for them to have separate bank accounts right from the beginning.

CANCER (21st June – 22nd July)

In everything that Cancer does, especially connected with love and money, 'security' is the basic motivation and drive. They see every penny that they earn and save, as a step towards owning their own home, buying a car, stocking up the refrigerator, and generally contributing to the welfare of their family. In courtship they may appear mean or cautious in their spending, as most of their money goes to help support other members of their family.

When they take on extra work to have the money to 'lavish' on their sweethearts, they ususally turn to jobs in the community that are particularly people-orientated; working at a local bar, restaurant, or hotel. Their big extravagances will be food, boxes of chocolates, cakes and frequently wine and liquor.

When they give their sweethearts presents, they are usually for the home. Items that can be stored for the big occasion, or added to the other treasures in the 'hope chest'. All household linens, pillows, rugs, china place settings, and cutlery, are high on their list. Dating will consist simply of visiting the cinema, or going out to a restaurant for a meal, even though they prefer to cook and serve at home.

As a wedding is so symbolic of love and the future family, they insist on a large scale celebration, yet may compromise by having the reception at the local church hall, or at the spacious home of a friend or relative. They will not leave anyone off the guest list. The food will be wholesome and plentiful and, to help with the costs, many of the wives will contribute to the preparation of the banquet. No one will go home hungry.

Most of Cancer's wages will be spent on setting up home, making it comfortable, charming and welcoming. Pets are a must, a dog and a cat. Until the children come along they dote on and spoil their kittens and puppies. Cancerians are exceptionally good at putting money aside for food, and for the payments on the house, and the furniture.

The decor is usually simple, but full of nostalgic momentos, and photographs – ancestors, school reunions, weddings and military experiences. Investment in antiques, heirlooms, silverware and paintings, will be another safe area for speculation.

While the clothes they buy are most practical, bought for wear rather than style, Cancerians are amongst some of the best-dressed people in the world. They know what to buy, what is good value, what is going to last, and what will have a touch-of-class look, even though bought at a bargain basement shop. They prefer to be comfortable and when dating, or going to an important function, they will first dress for comfort.

They'll have lots of children and spend lots of money on them, they want them to be happy and healthy. A tendency to over feed their children can become a problem, as they tend to be over-weight and to keep holding on to that extra fat all through schooldays, like their Cancerian parent. Cancerians hate to throw away anything that can be recycled, or reused. They carefully repair and paint toys, wash and take care of clothes that can be handed down from one child to another.

Cancerians rarely divorce, they are tenacious and want to hold on to their loved ones for ever, even when the time has come to part. Financially they want to organise everything so that the whole family is protected, that no one should want, or do without vital life sustaining items. As most Cancerians remain friendly with their divorced spouses, and continue to take an active interest in the children's education and welfare, there are usually no legal problems . . . only emotional ones.

LEO (23rd July – 22nd -August)
When Leos are in love, or in the process of falling in love, nothing is too good for their loved ones. They will buy the biggest diamond for their girl friend, or the fastest sports car for their boy friend. Being the royal sign of the zodiac, Leos bring their grand and generous qualities into the relationship.

Money, which miraculously appears whenever they need it, just slips through their fingers. A night out on the town will include the best table in the best restaurant, a champagne dinner, musicians serenading at the table, and the limousine waiting to take them on to the next stop. Even when times are tight, Leo will go through the same ritual, but not quite so often. They are show offs, and they love it, especially when they think it is making their loved one happy.

Everyone who is anyone will want to attend Leo's wedding, so consider the enormous bill at the end an investment. Still, they won't forget their less wealthy friends and acquaintances – they want everyone to be there. The nearest thing to a hit West End musical will be the wedding itself. The choir, the speeches, the flowers, the unusual number of ushers and bridesmaids, and the most elegant and chic clothes of the bride and groom.

Setting up home, whether a one bedroom flat, or a mansion, will be amazingly economical. Leos have the ability to give the appearance of richness and prosperity by finding items that give a theatrical effect. They love to find really old pieces of furniture, frames and decorative works of art in junk shops, or in remote towns, then clean them up, restore them and put them on show. Their home is a showplace . . . their stage.

When it comes to divorce, there is just as much drama, expense and publicity, as when they got married. They turn from being the royal beast of the jungle, generously handing out gifts and money to their family and loved ones, into the alley cat, spitefully denying their former loved ones those things due to them. Remember their pride will be hurt, and they will do everything, proper and improper, to keep their self image . . . or to get revenge!

VIRGO (23rd August – 22nd September)
Traditionally frugal and cautious, Virgos are more likely to buy their loved ones items for the office, or for their work, than jewellery and other adornments. But to be fair, when Virgo is in love, he or she will do anything to make their sweetheart happy – even if it means fighting their basic

instincts and delving into their pockets or purses.

Hardworking Virgos always have a way to make extra money. They love to work, and will usually spend more of their free time and leisure hours working. It works out well when they find a romantic partner who shares this same interest, and with their combined energies they will make a financial killing.

They spend most of their money on their career, and during their courtship days have very little money to splash around at the usual bars, dance halls and theatres. Somehow they do come up with imaginative and romantic ideas, picnics in secluded places of natural beauty, walks along the beach at sunset, working together for some social cause in the community . . . things that don't involve spending money.

Their weddings are usually the smallest, involving just the two principals and a witness. Why spend (waste) money on a wedding? Though many notable Virgos have had spectacular marriage feasts, they tend to resent the money it costs. They would rather put that money into a new business.

It is wonderful what ideas a Virgo will come up with when setting up home. The home is practical, and usually spotlessly clean. Virgos love the crystals, whites and pure pastel tints, and will surround themselves with objects and furniture that always looks elegant and dignified. Yet one room must be put aside for all the books, papers, files and other paraphernalia that they have accumulated over the years.

Babies interfere with the work schedule and so tend to come later in the marriage. However, they do take great care of their children, and would rather spend money on education than on clothes and toys – unless they are educationally motivated toys. They buy books by the cart-load!

During divorce procedures, should this occur, Virgo will be more than fair. They are not possessive of property or furnishings. They may feel attached to their papers and books, and can easily walk out of the investment of time and money, and start again. They will methodically itemise and list all the joint holdings and share the property right down the middle.

LIBRA (23rd September – 22nd October)

So romantic, Libra spends more money on love and romance than most of the other signs (except Leo, of course). First of all they want to look good; they are already good looking, and charming, so why not dress the best. They love to surround themselves with objects that indicate *love* – crystal hearts, roses, photos of old sweethearts, and children, and like to give romantic gifts to their loved ones.

Dating will consist of attending the opera and the ballet, the latest West End play, and supporting social and charitable dinner-dances. As they are always willng to lend a hand Librans find themselves on the committees of many community functions, and 'spend a lot of their spare time helping to sell tickets, and assist in the preparations for the special events. This is where they most likely met their sweetheart and their mutual interests broadened their love for each other.

The wedding while not necessarily being extravagant will be costly, the clothes will be designed by a famous dress maker and the choice of venue for the reception will be chic and socially acceptable. Often a Libra will have a little present or souvenir for all the guests to remind them of this happy event.

Setting up home is really no problem, once the decisions have been made about paint colours, wallpaper designs, and the general overall look that the couple want. Libra's indecisiveness disappears in the home, they know what they want and are willing to demand it. As they want their home to look beautiful from the very first day, then they are going to put a lot of money into it, even if it means buying on credit.

As children are very important to Librans, they tend to have babies early in the marriage. Librans tend to look younger all through their life, and having a young family while they are young, helps them to grow together. Somehow, while they want their children to have everything, there is a tendency not to spend much money themselves; they have a knack of getting others, relatives and friends, to buy things for the children.

Divorce is nerve-wracking for Libra. They are the sign of the balance and to be suddenly thrown off-balance and to have to re-adjust themselves in the world without their dearly beloved is difficult. Libra tends to be too selfish and demanding in the settlement, they want it all; even though they are moderate and loving, when in love they can become very vindictive and inconsiderate. Usually the only way to settle a separation or divorce of a Libran and their spouse, is through the courts.

SCORPIO (23rd October – 22nd November)
When it comes to love and money you can never really be sure what is on Scorpio's mind. Whilst they are romantics their motivations are so devious and convoluted that while wining and dining with their sweetheart they may really be plotting a big business deal. The ring that he, or she, gives to the loved one, could be the spoils of illegal smuggling or merely the treasured heirloom of a recently departed aunt. They appear to be spending a lot of money, and yet they will not tell their sweetheart what they do for a living, or how much money they have in the bank.

You can be sure that they will have a most exciting time during courtship, with all sorts of crazy, bizarre and unusual activities. Due to their personality, which is dynamic, mysterious, and appealing, they seem to be able to find restaurants that give them a complimentary meal or friends who send them free passes for the latest hit play or film. So, generally, their actual outlay on romance is much less than would appear on the surface.

The wedding will also be equally economical, but as many friends and colleagues from the past want to help (for some friendly or sinister reason) the affair is likely to be big. Not elegant, chic or fashionable, but wonderfully full of life, sensual and emotional. When it comes to a second marriage, they may forget the formalities and simply get married secretly at a registry office, or at a quiet chapel well out of town.

The home will be full of the most amazing antique furniture and tend towards the traditional rather than the ultra modern. It will looked lived in, and Scorpio will be just as happy with secondhand furniture as brand new sofas, tables or chairs. They can always sense a sale, or a bargain.

Babies come and go with Scorpio. They may be the father of many more children than indicated by the present family, and they will happily pay for their 'mistake' as they're philanthropic and loving. The Scorpio mother has been known to have her children adopted, due to social or economic difficulties at the time of the child's birth. Yet those that have hung on to their babies, through storms and depressions, have been able to bring them up on a shoe-string to be healthy, well-educated and happy, to the amazement of all.

In a divorce there are so many complications that both parties may spend years fighting over who will get what. Once a divorce has been announced – then it is the survival of the fittest. They would rather burn down the estate and give the family jewels to charity, than feel that they have to hand over a penny to their ex.

SAGITTARIUS (23rd November – 21st December)
Sagittarius is the big gambler, the big wheeler-dealer, and will invest a lot of time and money in their sweethearts. They have great style, and are not afraid to let other people see their expansive generosity, and their expensive jewellery and

accessories. Much of their petty cash comes from winning at the track, or at cards, or a surprise repayment of an investment made in a friend's showbusiness venture, or a local boutique. Sagittarians love the risks and chances in life, and somehow they win more than they lose.

To list the things that Sagittarius will spend money on during a courtship would be like reprinting the dictionary – everything! Whatever their boy friend or girl friend desires will be granted. It is no surprise that Santa Claus appears on the streets and in the department stores during the time of Sagittarius! Presents from Sagittarius to their loved one usually include cameras, movie making equipment, air line tickets and jogging wear. They like active gifts that means action and adventure in the relationship.

They are more likely to get married at a ski lodge high in the mountains, or at a prestigious health club, where there can be lots of beer drinking, college songs, and rowdy behaviour. They dislike spending money on traditional or conservative events, they prefer something spontaneous and different. Even the honeymoon will be very unconventional, perhaps a hiking trip, or a trip to some obscure country to help the deprived. Yes, they do spend money on their wedding but not much, more is spent getting to and from the honeymoon than on the actual nuptials.

When they set up a home it's a simple one. They will purchase utilitarian furniture, 'for the time being', and camp out for the first few years. As they don't spend much time at home any way, why should they do it up? The house may be large with a big garden but not much will be done to the little used living room.

Babies are not always planned, they would interfere with the freedom so necessary to Sagittarius, but when they do have a family they like their children to be sporty and outgoing. They will happily spend money on sports equipment, camping and fishing trips, riding lessons at the local horse stables, and skiing holidays. Education is important to them, but they will find ways of getting their children to win scholarships, and to get grants.

Divorce is difficult, as they spend so much time in finding the right partner, that they feel it is failure to lose in love. It is this attitude that makes the division of property difficult. They may want to hang on to certain items, furniture or property for no apparently good reason. Their logic during a divorce doesn't make sense and their judgement about money matters is totally off balance, therefore a lawyer, or judge, may have to make the decisions. The expansive, generous person disappears, a nervous, scheming and miserly 'Scrooge' takes over. They just hate to lose!

CAPRICORN (22nd December – 19th January)

Capricorns in love spend a lot but are not generous. They will take their date to the most expensive restaurant in town, show off to the other successful business tycoons present, use the limousine for a one block trip, yet will hate to tip reasonably and grumble about the price of the best wine in the house.

They love to show their loved ones how much they love them, and have been known to shower cars, diamonds, watches, and other expensive items on their lovers. Romance and love are expensive. But as most Capricorns are in a position to demand good salaries and some inherit wealth, this extravagance in the pursuit of love doesn't hurt their bank balance very much.

Power is important to them. To have power over their loved one, or to make their sweetheart see them as 'powerful' figures in the community, is a daily discipline. Politicians at heart, they know just what to do to impress and sway the emotions of their loved one with no expense spared.

Their wedding is one of elegance and prestige and will be a diplomatic coup for them, getting people together who may not have seen or spoken to each other for years.

Their home will be large and spacious with plenty of security and burglar-proof alarms, filled with antiques and family heirlooms, portraits and mementos. They will want a large garden where they can spend many relaxing hours, thinking and contemplating. Gardening becomes a major expense in this household, so, too, do dogs, cats and other pets.

Capricorns certainly don't spoil their children, they can be mean and tight when the child wants anything, whether toys, clothes or books. They want the child to develop economic drive and will encourage them to make money doing odd jobs for the family and neighbours. But they like their children to have a university or college education, and will scrimp and save to make sure their child becomes a doctor, a lawyer, or a professor.

Divorce can be a messy business involving a lot of legal work. Even though a judge may declare that something must be done, if Capricorn decides that it is unjust, then there will be further lengthy legal hassles. Many things will be said in this divorce that will be hurtful and insulting. Capricorns suffer, and will be willing to pay to make their former spouse suffer too.

AQUARIUS (20th January – 19th February)
Somehow love and money don't seem to motivate Aquarians as much as they do other signs. They can be extremely shrewd in money matters and great lovers, yet the intellect and sincerity of a relationship are paramount. It is possible for Aquarians to go through their courtship and not spend a penny. They would walk, or bicycle, with their sweetheart to the library, museum or to the local television studio, where they would spend many hours doing research.

Strangely enough they are wonderful at raising money for popular causes, and will hand over vast amounts they have collected, but hate to part with their well earned money. And being practical and using their great initiative they can go through life on a very low budget.

Of course there are Aquarians who do spend money on their love life, but they are very few, and far between, and then there's an underlying motivation for it. They like to travel with their sweethearts, especially by fast cars, or commercial airlines, to explore exotic lands, and set up international businesses. Some even manage to get some government office to give them a grant for such 'educational' adventures. When they give gifts, they like to give the latest electronic invention, things that may be far ahead of the times, video-discs, special computers, calculators, and television accessories and recording devices. When they give, they give big!

As they are likely to get married on the back of two llamas, while on excavation in Afghanistan, or perilously balancing on top of a mountain, by the local holyman, they can get away by giving a big tip. And the more conventional marriages cost very little – a few select friends with home-made sandwiches and an imaginatively designed wedding cake will suffice.

Their home will either be the most ultra-modern, full of futuristic paintings, large over-stuffed cushions for lounging, intricate lighting designs and sound systems, or chock-full of old newspapers, books and family heirlooms and antiques that have been dumped on them.

Babies? What babies? It seems that Aquarians don't have them. Or if they do you never see them around the house. In all sorts of weather, good and bad they will be suitable wrapped up and put out into the fresh air on the porch. Babies interfere too much with their schedule. Yet when they start to speak and become more independent then Aquarians take a special interest, directing them immediately to the library of books, pencils, crayons and paper. They'll insist their child gets the best of education, at home and at school, and will go without themselves to make sure they enjoy the benefits of further education.

Divorce is easy and efficient. They like their freedom in any case and so are never really bothered by separations from their loved ones. They are smart enough to know that 'when it's over, it's over', and while they may remain friends, there aren't the terrible emotional ties and heartaches that other signs of the zodiac suffer. A quick divorce, and settlement is always fair, usually fifty-fifty.

PISCES (20th February – 20th March)

Pisces are so much in love that money just slips through their fingers, almost until there is nothing left. They will give their last penny to their lovers for they are truly the martyr when it comes to romance. So this becomes a terribly expensive and hard working period of their life, money being the token by which they can prove how much they love their boyfriend or girlfriend. If necessary they will work overtime, take on a second job, in order to have enough money to keep their loved one happy. As many Pisces work in hospitals and other service orientated jobs there is always a demand for their talents and skills.

In courtship, nothing will be left out, the weekly bouquet of roses, the perfumed notes, little trinkets and gifts given at every meeting, dining out, dining at home, the best wines, the best boxes of chocolates, the works ... And either their bank accounts, or credit cards give out way before their love.

The wedding will be traditional, with the religious ceremony their parents had when they got married, and their parents before them. The reception will be large but not necessarily expensive. Good food, plenty of drink, and lots of dancing, with music by a local band. As Pisces have done so many good turns in the past, many people will donate food, liquor, flowers, and their services at a time like this to show their appreciation, and to help the newly-weds on their way.

Setting up their home will be no problem at all – it will have a basically traditional setting, with economically priced, but very attractive furnishings. Pisces have no need of expensive works of art, they are not materialistic, but they will be surrounded by beauty, whether plants and flowers or cleverly placed posters and prints. Being artistic and theatrical in their approach to decorating their home, it will be a surprise to others how little can be spent to achieve such effects. _

Pisces love children, want a large family and will dote upon them from the moment of birth. During school days they never allow their child to go without and will encourage them to take painting, music and dancing lessons. They want their child to be a movie star.

Most Pisces don't divorce, they would rather suffer and be the martyr than to separate. Yet many do get divorced and there are usually many tears and emotions before the property and money is properly divided. Pisces want to hang on to all the family mementos and, more than likely, the kids too.

Chapter Ten
The next twenty years – a psychic look ahead

This is an attempt to divine, by an interpretation of planetary movement, the fiscal fortunes of the globe over the next two decades. Inevitably, prediction on such a scale is difficult and we don't pretend to be able to see more than general trends – in some years more than others! And when we refer to 'you' we mean the general reader, whatever star sign he or she may belong to. For the next seven years communications and travel will be unpredictable, there will be many sudden changes and happenings due to political changes throughout the world, trade unions will use their powers in slowing down the trains, buses and other means of transport, and affecting the presses. Many newspapers will go out of business. Still, there will be a general feeling of determination; and people will become more self-sufficient and independent. With this new attitude to life, and to the political structure, a sense of optimism will grow.

After November 28, 1981, people will start cutting down on overheads, extravagant habits, and by searching out new ways to make money, will be generally luckier than before. Gambling will become a big source of tax income for the government as well as for the individual. Investments, speculation and risky jobs will be more tempting in the future, as many of our 'safe' investments and 'secure' jobs disappear in front of our eyes. Many large corporations will merge with others during this period, to give themselves strength in unity. Even international treaties will be more important, and many nations will be making long term treaties and alliances, while others will be hostile. The world of traditional diplomacy, consulates and embassies will begin to deteriorate. Relationships with foreign countries will have to be looked at in a different light. The propaganda, history and myths associated with attitudes towards the greater world powers, and their former colonies and protectorates, will start to break down over the next few years. Old spiritual and religious values will have to be taken into consideration in international affairs. There will be a sense of honesty and truth allied to open hostility towards national enemies. The days of the cold war are gone. Little nations are now able to negotiate with larger nations, as the world's natural resources appear to be given to those who need the strongest trump card at the bargaining table. This philosophy will extend to the small businessman making deals with former big monopolies and industrial empires.

1982   Many of the trends of 1981 continue. Generally a happy and daring time for most people trying to make the most of their savings and investments. There appears to be more winning than losing, and the overall feeling of the individual will be that of 'beating the system'. Business partnerships, and merging of conglomerates, are still the vital force, yet still keeping individual freedom and independence. As the value of currency becomes more and more unpredictable, many big organisations, as well as individuals will invest in property, precious stones and metals, and in independent means of travel and communication. This is the year of the big-time entrepreneur, and big-time projects.

This is also a year to clean all the skeletons out of the closets. There will be a universal soul cleansing. Many crimes, and immoral practices, perpetrated all over the world, often in the name of law and order, religion, and human rights, will be brought to light. Political criminals will be brought to justice, and this will have a big influence on the stock market. Even in one's own corporations, societies, clubs and work places, there will be no place for the guilty to hide. This trend to honesty will make business dealings easier to handle. Contracts will be less complicated and businessess will save on legal expenses and overheads. You will see a more serious and practical attitude towards money after November 30, 1982. The risks that people took earlier in the year will finally pay off, but the feeling of speculation may be a little bit more cautious. Dying will become less of a burden. Funerals, cremation and burial, while still under the auspices of religious organisations will become government controlled, due to health restrictions. Death expenses will be as reasonable as birth expenses to the family.

1983   International and long distance business matters continue to bring luck. You will be tempted to travel more than ever before, and all sorts of wonderful offers, cheap travel and business expense-paid trips, will become commonplace to you. From an optimistic point of view, while you may get rid of unsuccessful or unproductive partners, and contracts, you will now be open to fill the vacuum made by their departure, by allying yourself with proven and well tested products and businesses. Expand whatever you do, this is a period of business 'colonialism'.

After November 6, 1983 money will be more available, and changes in the tax laws may make it easier on prize winners, inheritors of legacies, insurance claimants and other financial beneficiaries. International travel will become cheaper.

1984   This is a year of many changes. Money may be made through radical ideas and inventions. Many industries and people involved with military supplies, weapons, ammunition, vehicles, transportation, clothing and recreational businesses for troops in other countries, will become rich. While this may not show a major war, there is a huge build-up of military strength on both sides. Weapons, and military investments will become the blue chip stocks in world trade, and in international negotiation. The price of gold will go higher. In the 1980s gold will reach a record $1,000 an ounce, and most likely during one of the tense periods associated with war in specific areas of the world.

A cautious eye should be maintained in all major business deals, especially until May 20, 1984. From that date until August 29, 1984 there will be much negotiation, and diplomatic discussion, on high and low levels. Treaties, contracts and partnerships will be able to be saved or signed during that time.

Meanwhile, many governments will discover oil and other resources in their own backyards. Shipping, businesses associated with the sea and the streamlining of the Navy will be a major concern of all politicians. Nevertheless, dishonest reports will deliberately mislead the general population, here and abroad. This is a year to carefully observe people in authority and especially our leaders. From January 19, 1984 until June 24, 1984 we must watch that we don't allow ourselves to be mislead by our partners, or our business colleagues.

1985   This is a good money-making period. In fact a big time business period for those whose ambitions are enormous, and whose energy level is high. Greed will be a motivating factor, but if profits are channelled into idealistic ventures methods won't be questioned.

The coalminers may have a better deal financially this year, but this will add another burden on the consumer, and industry, thereby the prices of goods will go up radically. Property will be a very lucrative business, and investment in one's own country will be rewarded by big profits. This expansive property period will be good for the buyer, and profitable for the seller.

After mid-November all foreign business affairs will have some difficulties. Keep an eye on foreign investments. Those that don't could be wiped out by government take-overs, revolutions, and other spontaneous outbursts of nationalism.

1986   A lot of luck plotting and planning takes place behind the scenes this year. Some may scheme, others will be preparing for the big burst of ambition and energy later on, the year. Sporting, games and speculative events will bring money and fun at the same time. Video-electronic fields are booming and television and computers are having an increased effect on business prosperity. There are many new electronic gadgets and techniques available to prospective employers.

1987   Big business ventures are making money rather than small ones. Dealing in art can be tricky, as there are many fakes around. However, the art world takes on a special magic this year. Business may take over from government in sponsoring artistic activity.

You will experience lots of changes with your travel plans, so keep a flexible schedule. There are many rewards to be gained working abroad, and working with foreign companies, and individuals. After March 3, 1987 you will feel expansive again. This is a good year to get things started, and to expand mental and financial horizons.

1988   Expect a lot of changes, influences from every source will have a major effect on your financial well-being so be prepared to flow with the tide and not to stay in a rut where you could be ruined, by political, social and economic trends. Keep your fingers into all projects, plans and businesses, they will all have ups and downs but in the final analysis people who stick to their guns will come out ahead.

You will notice many new tempting offers and opportunities after February 14, 1988. This is the year to start your own business, take over the presidency of the corporation, and to have a big promotion at work. The most influential time will be before May 28, 1988. After December 10, 1988 rewards and benefits are there to be gathered – this could bring financial income for many years to come.

1989   If you remember that success comes only from hard work you cannot fail. Occasionally things will drop into your lap, but generally speaking it is perseverance and application that pays off in the long run. Look forward to a hard working, but successful period; decisions have already been made, and it would be wise to keep to your schedule.

Think *big*, and keep away from petty enterprises, unless you consider them hobbies. After March 12, 1989 there will be luck with all promotional, educational and advertising business, until July 31, 1989, at which time property matters will start yielding big rewards. Look at buildings, houses, restaurants, hotels and see what you could do to turn them into cash for your bank account. Many will make money from the real estate negotiations, others buying and selling, some by redecorating and restoring.

Older members of the family should be consulted and involved in proposed plans, they have some sound advice, having gone through similar circumstances themselves.

The secret is to have many things going on this year. The odds are against failure and with the right attitude and enthusiasm there is a lot of money to be made.

1990   There won't be too many changes this year. The trends of the past couple of years continue, with success still associated with ambitions and career. It is a time when many people will be considering what is their true vocation and what simply their job. You must nevertheless go after your true goals, your vocation in life. There are many planetary influences helping you to attain your goal and government funded programmes are now available for people to put into action their big-time career ambitions.

Try to get all real estate and property matters organised before August 19, 1990. Make sure all loose ends are tied up in connection with home and family affairs, while they can benefit you. Adventure, speculation, big risks are in the air – you could win a great deal in the last half of the year, but you could easily become careless and extravagant and lose a lot too.

Romance plays a bigger part than usual and you will have fun, while making money. Take along your loved one to business conventions, and you will have success as a team.

Romance should not be allowed to stand in the way of success professionally. If it creates unnecessary pressures other plans should be made. All personal relationships should be fun this year, not heartaches.

1991   Image and public appearance is now more important than before. The general trend will be to judge people by their friends, clothes and their environment. While as an individual you may have felt that these standards are false, and in most cases this is true, we are now in a period of tense political, social and economic competition, and these superficial trappings are very important. However, there will be no open 'witch hunts'. People will fight for their beliefs in the material world, but at this time in history, there will be strong pressure to go along with the trend, and hope that within a short time this will pass.

There will be money to be made in all showbusiness type ventures, television, radio, theatre, fashion, public relations, medical-health related businesses, health foods, diets, health clubs, clothing and fashion, cosmetics and other consumer products. This will be a year of success through service to others and a willingness to compromise in order to attain goals.

1992   Work established in 1991 continues to be successful. Never get your mind away from big business, as it takes the same amount of energy and time to get a small business or boutique going, as it does to work hand in hand with large corporate organisations.

This is not a year to follow advice from friends and well-wishers, follow your own hunches, just make sure your are not being self deceptive.

Partnerships become more important after October 11, 1992, and you could add to your number of partners, or contractual associates, team mates, and business deals, or you could spend the same amount of intensity with romantic and love partners.

Changes of status for religious organisations, and

charitable or tax exempt status corporations, will affect all churches, synagogues and other religious groups, educational foundations and pseudo-artistic centres. All tax shelters will probably be eliminated, and taxes will be more fairly collected. This, of course, could have a big effect on many of you, and other means of investment should be considered.

Like other people, you will most likely be working a four day week, with plenty of leisure time. Electronics play a more important part in your daily schedule, and you may be able to leave much of your work, and your responsibilities to electronic equipment programmed to your particular skills.

Security will be based on voice tones and body prints preparing everyone for credit changes and new systems of banking. Codes and deposits will be automatic by then. Payments of debts, and credit payments and considerations will be based on life-long credit rating, secured by life insurance.

1993   Drastic changes in the world's currency systems begin to usurp traditional methods. World trade will be manipulated through a world bank, and through controls in several centres of the different continents. We will enter a two year period of new lessons in government and trade despite radical opposition to the major improvements. There will be one world currency system for international trade. Most people will go along with the government's wishes, others will form committees and lobbying groups. Nationalism will be strong in most countries.

The next two years will be the most difficult for a long time, you may lose money on some things, yet make money on others. You will have to re-evaluate what you want out of your working life, and while the decisions may be difficult, you will come out of this period much wiser for the experience.

The period of soul-searching starts during May 22, 1993 to July 1, 1993, and continues throughout 1994. Try to get everything up to date by then, so that your files, accounts and special investments will be protected and it will be easier to go from one system to another.

After July 1, 1993, you will know who your friends are, and who may be counted as a rival and even an enemy. There will be drastic shake-ups in government, so be super-aware of what is going on, keep up to date with your information sources. Remember you are investing in the future, forget the old values, and start fitting in with the 21st Century methods and ideals.

Spend money on art, jewellery and precious metals, computers and means of transport. Antiques, even in the modern world, will take on greater value, and will be very negotiable.

1994 Plotting and planning behind the scenes will foster many deceptive business practices and everyone will have to watch out for confidence tricksters and racketeers. However, the overall view of business continues to be good, but you must be aware of economic forces that you could easily ignore, or forget. You will be wise to buy land, property and other valuable assets, rather than rely on banks, and saving accounts.

A new system for electing our leaders will be put into action, and many new parties will be formed. Mini-governments will be set up to control designated areas of the country, and computerised video systems will enable the various centres to interlock and have discussions via the television media. This will save travel time, and other government expenses, and also be available for the residents of the different areas to know exactly what is being said by their own elected officers and other officials.

The feeling that Big Brother is watching you, will be prevalent during this time, while various methods of surveillance are tested for security of homes, offices and banks. There will be strict government control and public vigilance of the government departments involved. January

29, 1994 starts a two year 'test period' when everyone will feel like a guinea pig. It will last until April 8, 1996.

1995   Just as everyone feels they are getting used to the new systems imposed upon them by their government, a year of turmoil and changes begins. Currency will be discontinued, a computerised system will actually go into effect later in the year. Heated discussions about finances start on January 17, 1995, and the debate continues until April 23, 1995 invoking spiritual values, philosophies and the research that has been taking place during recent years. Traditionalists will want to hang on to coins, notes and cheques. Crime prevention organisations and the government will favour a credit card systems, instant banking methods, and electronically controlled payment of bills. Freedom of financial expression is on its way out.

New and efficient means of travel will be heavily financed by the tax payer, and most correspondence will be done via TV screens, and satellites. Information can be typed in, or shown to a camera at one location, and printed out and read at the other on the television set itself.

More people will travel in 1995 than any other year in history. Many in search of a new home, others on spending sprees to buy things in other countries. Many will find it cheaper to take package tours than to stay at home. So the travel industry will be a big business to consider, to make your fortune at this time. Of course, you could invest in your own jet.

By Nobember 10, 1995, the new currency system will be installed. From April 2, 1995 until June 10, 1995, we will see more home use of electronic computers. Most homes will be installed with one and they will become as common as the refrigerator and the telephone. Computers will contain all our private documents and information, retrievable only by the individuals themselves.

Many homeowners will have their own source of energy and solar heating will be in nearly every home in the country.

This will save individuals enormous amounts of money, and will balance the old usage of oil, coal, and other fuels for heat, and electricity. Water will also become a valuable commodity, and each community will be responsible for pollution, and the supply of un-contaminated drinking water. Many homes will have drinking water delivered to them, as milk was in the past.

On June 10, 1995 a big shake up in the government will affect the stock market world wide. Many people will consider moving to other towns and cities, and some to other countries. There will be mass exoduses from some polluted and over-crowded areas.

1996   People will still be thinking over the many changes of lifestyle that they have gone through. It will bring the best out in everyone and the anticipation starts the year off with much energy for everyone. By January 13, 1996, the electronic revolution will have taken place. Doors will open electronically by the sound of a person's voice, messages will be spoken as you enter the door by an electronic secretary, and meals prepared by an electronic cook.

Religion and individual faiths and philosophies once again will be popular, as there will be more free time for personal recreation and self development. Higher consciousness will be developed in the school system, and subjects such as astrology, tarot card reading, hypnosis and other metaphysical or mental disciplines will be as common as arithmetic and English literature.

Now that money has been practically eliminatd, you will always seem to have more than enough in your computerised credit bank to do everything you want to do, and more. And you will always be able to get additional credit to expand, and to improve property and business facilities.

1997   This year could slip by with hardly anyone noticing. This is not the time to make the big changes, it is more a time to relax and have fun. Buy the things you have dreamed about and take out time for holidays, and other leisure activities. By now you may be enjoying a three day week, and four day weekends. There is not much work for you to do, and the electronic helpers and overseers will keep you informed if your services are needed.

After January 22, 1997 you enter this relaxing and social time. Despite this freedom, you will take things more seriously, there will be very little excuse for carelessness, and justice will be meted out equally. The slightest apparent error, or fraudulent entry (even by accident) in your computer bank, may be punished by a heavy fine, automatically deducted from your account, with no judge or jury to protect you. There will be no appeals.

People will do business with the government, and the control will enable most people to get on with their work in a less hampered and less formal way.

1998   As the end of the 1900s starts to get closer, we may see the end of many practices in business and finance that we grew up with. While we see the practicality and efficiency of this, it is hard to break away from the nostalgic and friendly ways of doing business in the past. Even business meetings may not be necessary any more.

We will nevertheless turn again to the sea for business ideas and discoveries. Medicine and cures for certain types of cancer will be discovered by 1998 in the sea, and super freighters will still be able to transport fuels, and other products cheaper than any other method.

Drugs and alcohol again become popular with the excess of free time, and the governments of the world may finally get involved in the drug traffic business formally, to control crime, and the suffering of those who cannot break the habit – and to help collect taxes from the profits of the contraband drug market. Many drugs forbidden in the past will be used in hospitals, and will be readily available by prescription, and through government agencies. The philosophy of the government may be to exercise control of the health industry, and to discourage individuals who resort to crime in order to purchase drugs or to sell them. As with alcohol, the government will collect large taxes from this business activity.

Sports and leisure activities will be a major source of income for anyone with a flair for entertaining people, and amusing them by offering them something unique to do. You may try out your ideas between January 29, 1998 and August 25, 1998, and if you feel enthusiastic about this new business, launch it after November 27, 1998.

While you may be fairly well organised and perhaps limited in what you can do for a couple of years, you will be doing a lot of planning this year. After February 12, 1998 you would be wise to do a lot of work in seclusion; if you announce your intentions too early you may miss opportunities later, other people may get annoyed or jealous, and you may lose interest. Keep exciting new plans secret.

Insurance companies will take on new areas of insurance, as automobile companies finally get their collision-proof cars into the market, and stolen items may be traced by bleepers. 1999   There will be a wonderful surge of interest in making money on a large scale. Tax laws will be changed again and with the changes of the political system in 1999, there will be more incentive again to make money for the individual.

The film and television industries will expand, and there will be increased encouragement from the government. Grants and loans will not be as difficult to obtain from the government and big business.

Eating habits will have drastically changed by the end of the century and nutrition will become more important than eating gourmet meals at fashionable restaurants. People will become more and more health conscious and restaurants will finally offer a choice of traditional meals, or healthy nutritional ones. The prices of foods will rise dramatically. You could therefore invest in the food business, or in the new nutritional supermarkert type chains across the country. As you may not be so concerned about adding to you bank balance as you once were, you may dabble in food as a sideline. There will be a need for it.

2000   As we enter the year 2000, we are consumed with the passion to learn and study more about the human psyche and what makes it tick. Education, special schools, and quick methods of learning languages and other subjects will be so efficient and computerised that this will be a major area of income for big business groups. Due to transportation difficulties and excessive costs, many children will study at home supervised by the television teacher. Means of transport will be revised and many large cities will have banned unnecessary private traffic from city centres. Public buses and other transportation, such as overhead tracks, and people-movers, will get a lot of government funding to expand their services. After August 10, 2000 the new transportation method will become safer and more efficient and by October 17, 2000 it will be already paying for itself in nearly all major cities.

The individual incentive is still the most magical way to look at finances. And by doing so one may make life fuller, more efficient and less boring. The economic necessities of the artist may make him create great works of art, and the greed of big businessmen and government leaders have often opened the doors to new and exciting inventions. Whatever the motivation, the next century promises ideas and thoughts never dreamed of in the history of mankind.

Appendix I
Lucky numbers

Many people go through life with one obstacle after another turning up. While it is normal to have a few obstacles, some people have more than their share. You might be one of them, and the reason could be something simple which may never have occurred to you ... your personal number.

Numbers rule everything, birthdays, addresses, telephone numbers, car license plates, social security, national health number, lottery tickets, age, army numbers and so on. Sometimes they are 'lucky', sometimes they are obstacles. Numerology, the study and interpretation of numbers, is an exacting science – but there are simple ways to find out your basic lucky number for yourself. You can determine whether a given day will be an auspicious one for you to sign a contract, make a major purchase or make a decision that is of obvious importance.

If you look over your life you will find that certain numbers, addresses, dates recur over and over again. Many people have found that by utilising their lucky number in gambling, speculation, and even bingo, they have more good fortune than at other times.

How to find your three lucky numbers:

1. The day of your birth e.g. 1st, 2nd, 3rd, etc. If your birthdate contains two numerals, add them together to make

just one. So for someone born on the 23rd of the month their lucky number would be (2 + 3 =) 5.

2. The numerical total of the entire birthdate. If you were born on 23rd September 1936, first express the date entirely in numerals e.g. 23.9.1936 then add each number to the next until you have just one number left:
2 + 3 + 9 + 1 + 9 + 3 + 6 = 33
3 + 3 = 6
So 6 would be the second lucky number for someone born on 23rd September 1936.

3. Your name number. Write down your entire name. You have several choices.
The full name given you at birth.
Your professional name.
The name your family calls you.
The name plus initials of first or middle names.
Try them all to see which one suits you best.
Under each letter write the corresponding number (1–9) from the Lucky Number Name Code.

Lucky Number Name Code

a b c d e f g h i j k l m n o p q r s t u v w x y z
1 2 3 4 5 6 7 8 9 1 2 3 4 5 6 7 8 9 1 2 3 4 5 6 7 8

Your name ____
Numbers   Total =

                                           ____

Reduce to single digit 1–9.

                                           ____

To really make a big success in life you need a *good* name not just a pretty sounding name (although that can help), or an executive name (that can add to your image), but a name that is conducive to success.

Preferably the name should correspond with your birthdate number. One number should match the other, 9–9 or 5–5.

Three very dramatic examples of world leaders' birthdays and names show how matching names and birthdays can add luck.

Prime Minister Margaret Thatcher was born October 13, 1925.
1. Birth number.   10.13.1925. digits add up to 22 = 4.
2. Name Number.   M a r g a r e t   T h a t c h e r
               4 1 9 7 1 9 5 2   2 8 1 2 3 8 5 9
                                   = 76 = 13 = 4.

   Familiar name. M a g g i e   T h a t c h e r
               4 1 7 7 9 5   2 8 1 2 3 8 5 9 = 71 = 8.

Margaret Thatcher is luckier than Maggie Thatcher, as it matches. However, Maggie Thatcher being an 8 is compatible to 4 (2 × 4 = 8).

Former President Jimmy Carter was born October 1, 1924.
1. Birth number.   10.1.1924. digits add up to 18 = 9.
2. Name number. J i m m y   C a r t e r
               1 9 4 4 7   3 1 9 2 5 9 = 54 = 9.
   Real name.   J a m e s   C a r t e r
               1 1 4 5 1   3 1 9 2 5 9 = 41 = 5.

Jimmy Carter is luckier than James Carter, as it matches. He wants to be recorded in history as being President Jimmy Carter not President James Carter.

President Ronald Regan was born February 6, 1911.
1. Birth number.   2.6.1911. digits add up to 20 = 2.
2. Name number. R o n a l d   R e a g a n
               9 6 5 1 3 4   9 5 1 7 1 5 = 56 = 11 = 2.
   Familiar name R o n n i e   R e a g a n
               9 6 5 5 9 5   9 5 1 7 1 5 = 67 = 13 = 4.

Ronald Reagan is luckier than Ronnie Reagan. However using
Ronnie is compatible as 4 is compatible to 2 (2 × 2 = 4)

P.M. Margaret Thatcher's
three lucky numbers are: Date– 4.
                                 Total– 4.
                                 Name–4.

President Jimmy Carter's
three lucky numbers are: Date– 1.
                                 Total– 9.
                                 Name–9.

President Ronald Reagan's
three lucky numbers are: Date– 6.
                                 Total– 2.
                                 Name–2.

Now what are yours?
Use your numbers to pick out lucky days of the month for you
to sign things, and to make important business and personal
moves.

Number 1   1st,   10th,   19th,   28th.
Number 2   2nd,   11th,   20th,   29th.
Number 3   3rd,   12th,   21st,   22nd.
Number 4   4th,   13th,   22nd,   31st.
Number 5   5th,   14th,   23rd.
Number 6   6th,   15th,   24th.
Number 7   7th,   16th,   25th.
Number 8   8th,   17th,   26th.
Number 9   9th,   18th,   27th.

Likewise, if gambling or signing a contract use an appropriate
time to match your number and the time you gamble, and the
amount too.

2:30 pm = 14:30 = 8. Bet number 8 or £8. Good for number
    8 people.
9:30 am = 12   = 3. Bet number 3 or £3. Good for number
    3 people.

How else you can use your lucky numbers.
1. Address of house or flat you are buying or renting.
2. Date to sign contracts, leases, application forms.
3. Dates or time, to send in the pools or other competitions.
4. Finding a compatible lover or spouse by their number.
5. Finding a compatible business partner by their number.
6. Raffle and lottery ticket number total.
7. You'll be able to think of hundreds of other ways ...

What kind of person are you by your number?
Read name number first. This is the real you that you show to
the public, family and friends using that name. Your total
birthdate number, if different, shows what you could be. It is
your life path number. Once you have checked your lucky
number, this is what it means:

NUMBER 1.
Is a powerful person, outgoing, flamboyant and loves to be in
the public eye. They are invincible and enter projects, places
and ideas 'where angels fear to tread'. They are leaders in their
field whatever they choose to do.

NUMBER 2.
People with this number love to do things in conjunction with
others. Team-mates at heart, they make marvellous romantic
lovers, but like two of everything – two jobs, two cars, two
loved ones (one may be their mother!). They are very cooperative, but need a partner to give themselves ambitious
drive.

NUMBER 3.
Is very stable. Overly conservative and easily embarrassed.
Very creative and communicates well. This is the number of
the trinity so this person tends to perfection. Cheerful and
optimistic. A tendency to be impatient but gets on well with
most people generally.

NUMBER 4.
Has great material luck, but tends to let their economic luck keep them in a rut. It is the number of security, and caution. Obstinate (but loyal), and very suspicious of others. Treats life a little too seriously. Needs to add a little more fun to their social and business life.

NUMBER 5.
The number of the traveller. Always able to find their way by instinct. Very impulsive and daring, loves changes and very unreliable at routine jobs, they make excellent actors, artists, writers and inventors. Good starters but hate to finish a job or project. Will live in many countries and often move home.

NUMBER 6.
Very harmonious and usually have excellent health, but can be hypochondriacs. Loves the family, and works best when given lots of responsibility. Good mediators, diplomats and judges. Loves dancing, music and the fine arts. Always looks young.

NUMBER 7.
Traditionally very lucky, but have many hold ups with career and marriage due to indecisiveness. Exceptionally intelligent, efficient but appears eccentric, also has a suspicious manner. Once they have set their mind on a goal they achieve their ambitions with honour.

NUMBER 8.
This is a very spiritual number, but also a very successful money-making person. Materialistic as well as religious. Extremely efficient, but wastes a lot of time making plans rather than doing. They boast over their money affairs and bargains. Success associated with churches and local organisations.

NUMBER 9.

Very philosophical, compatible with every other number, noble in attitude to life, and reaps general good fortune. Very charitable and involved with humanity. They are 'plain clothes hippies' at heart. They make excellent doctors, as well as social workers, and many entertainers have this number.

Appendix II
The best times for negotiation

It seems that there are cycles for every human activity, notwithstanding the signing and negotiations of financial deals and contracts. Whether you are buying or selling your property, collecting insurance, asking for a raise, loan or grant, or entering into new money-making partnerships, there is an uncanny recurrence that indicates astrologically that certain months are better for some sign's finances than for others.

Here is an easy-to-follow listing of the most important money deals, and the best months to attempt to reach an arrangement.

1. Buying or selling your home and property

	1st Choice	*2nd Choice*
ARIES:	June and July	April
TAURUS:	July and August	May
GEMINI:	August and September	June
CANCER:	September and October	July
LEO:	October and November	August
VIRGO:	November and December	September
LIBRA:	December and January	October
SCORPIO:	January and February	November
SAGITTARIUS:	February and March	December
CAPRICORN:	March and April	January
AQUARIUS:	April and May	February
PISCES:	May and June	March

2. Signing contracts and entering into partnerships
ARIES: June and October
TAURUS: July and November
GEMINI: August and December
CANCER: September and January
LEO: October and February
VIRGO: November and March
LIBRA: December and April
SCORPIO: January and May
SAGITTARIUS: February and June
CAPRICORN: March and July
AQUARIUS: April and August
PISCES: May and September

3. Investing, speculating and gambling
ARIES: August
TAURUS: September
GEMINI: October
CANCER: November
LEO: December
VIRGO: January
LIBRA: February
SCORPIO: March
SAGITTARIUS: April
CAPRICORN: May
AQUARIUS: June
PISCES: July

4. Starting business ventures, liquidating assets, dealing in
property and stocks and shares, starting a savings programme,
and organising finance
ARIES: May
TAURUS: June
GEMINI: July
CANCER: August
LEO: September

VIRGO:	October
LIBRA:	November
SCORPIO:	December
SAGITTARIUS:	January
CAPRICORN:	February
AQUARIUS:	March
PISCES:	April

5. Benefits from wills, legacies, inheritance and heirlooms, selling and buying antiques, doweries, grants, loans and gifts of money, insurance benefits, life insurance

ARIES:	November
TAURUS:	December
GEMINI:	January
CANCER:	February
LEO:	March
VIRGO:	April
LIBRA:	May
SCORPIO:	June
SAGITTARIUS:	July
CAPRICORN:	August
AQUARIUS:	September
PISCES:	October

Appendix III
Times to avoid

Over the years astrologers have discovered that the movements of the planet Mercury can have an adverse effect on business affairs. We would advise you not to sign contracts or start new business enterprises on the following dates:

1981	October 8	–	October 28
1982	January 24	–	February 14
	May 22	–	June 15
	September 20	–	October 12
1983	January 8	–	January 29
	May 3	–	May 27
	September 3	–	September 26
	December 23	–	January 12
1984	April 13	–	May 7
	August 16	–	September 8
	December 6	–	December 26
1985	March 26	–	April 18
	July 29	–	August 22
	November 20	–	December 9
1986	March 8	–	March 31
	July 11	–	August 4
	November 3	–	November 23
1987	February 20	–	March 15
	June 22	–	July 16
	October 18	–	November 7

1988	February 3	–	February 25
	June 2	–	June 26
	September 30	–	October 21
1989	January 17	–	February 7
	May 13	–	June 6
	September 13	–	October 5
1990	January 2	–	January 21
	April 24	–	May 18
	August 27	–	September 19
	December 16	–	January 5
1991	April 6	–	April 29
	August 9	–	September 2
	November 30	–	December 19
1992	March 18	–	April 10
	July 21	–	August 14
	November 12	–	December 2
1993	March 2	–	March 24
	July 3	–	July 27
	October 27	–	November 16
1994	February 12	–	March 6
	June 14	–	July 8
	October 10	–	October 31
1995	January 27	–	February 17
	May 25	–	June 18
	September 23	–	October 15
1996	January 11	–	January 31
	May 5	–	May 29
	September 5	–	September 28
	December 25	–	January 14
1997	April 16	–	May 10
	August 18	–	September 11
	December 9	–	December 28
1998	March 29	–	April 21
	August 2	–	August 25
	November 22	–	December 12

1999	March 11	-	April 3
	July 14	-	August 7
	November 6	-	November 26
2000	February 23	-	March 16
	June 24	-	July 19
	October 20	-	November 10